Campbell's
MICROWAVE COOKBOOK

CAMPBELL MICROWAVE INSTITUTE

PUBLICATIONS INTERNATIONAL, LTD.

This edition was prepared by the Publications Center and the
Campbell Microwave Institute, Campbell Soup Company, Campbell
Place, Camden, NJ 08103-1799.

Editors: Julia Malloy, Flora E. Szatkowski
Recipe Coordinators: Barbara A. Lynch, Dorcas B. Reilly
Home Economists: Jennifer L. Andersen, Elaine M. Gagliardi,
Rose M. Smith-Brydon
Canadian Recipe Consultant: Joan Fielden
Canadian Project Consultant: Stephen W. Krane
Photographers: William R. Houssell, Nancy B. Principato,
Maggie Wochele
Art Director: Warren Neal
Photo Coordinator: Jacqueline Finch
Food Stylists: Elizabeth J. Barlow, Maria J. Soriano
Accessories Stylist: Kathryn B. Foden

CAMPBELL MICROWAVE INSTITUTE
Susan Whittier, Director—Marketing
Marsha Cade, Communications Center
Peter Dakich, Media Services
Bob Fisher, Microwave Product Development
Paul D. Garwood, Microwave Packaging Development
Stan H. Kwis, Microwave Product Development
Barbara A. Lynch, Creative Food Center
Megan McNichols, Communications Center
Kevin J. Murphy, Sales Planning
Scott Noar, Microwave Product Development
Ravi Parmeswar, Microwave Product Development
William P. Piszek, Marketing Research
Charles E. Schick, Promotions
Frederick E. Simon, Ph.D., Microwave Packaging Research

On the front cover: Glazed Stuffed Cornish Hens (see page 40).
On the back cover from top to bottom: Cheesecake Pie (see page 148), Salmon Steaks in Dill Sauce (see page 46) and Country Captain (see page 30).

ISBN: 0-88176-744-1

This edition published by:
Publications International, Ltd.
7373 North Cicero Avenue
Lincolnwood, Illinois 60646

Printed and bound in Yugoslavia
h g f e d c b a

Contents

4

Campbell, Your Microwave Oven and You

The microwave oven has revolutionized the way we cook, and to some extent, the way we live. The fast-cooking, fast-cleanup qualities of microwave cooking fit right into the nonstop lifestyles of today's busy families. In little more than two decades, the microwave oven has earned a place in a majority of Canadian homes.

The resulting cooking revolution presents an exciting challenge. Whether you've cooked with a microwave oven for only a few weeks or a few years, you'll probably agree there's more to learn every day. There are new food products and packages, cookware and utensils to discover. The makers of paper towels, plastic wrap and foil are coming out with new ways to use those kitchen aids for cooking. And the products you've relied on for years offer microwave heating directions so you can use them with confidence.

What makes microwave cooking so special? First, of course, is the speed with which it heats and cooks food. Before the microwave oven, who ever dreamed that a five-minute baked potato was possible! Or that hamburger could be thawed in less time than it takes to fire up a grill!

Your microwave oven is second only to your dishwasher in helping you clean up, too. You can cook and serve frozen dinners in their throw-away containers and heat soup in its serving bowl. Because cooking utensils stay relatively cool, food doesn't stick to them as readily as in conventional cooking methods.

Microwave cooking tends to be low-fat cooking, good for calorie-watchers. Because microwave cooking is like steaming, it's also a particularly good way to prepare vegetables and fish and to reheat casseroles and other foods you want to remain moist.

Finally, as you'll learn from this book and your own experience, the microwave oven provides a host of new shortcuts and problem solvers, such as melting butter, thawing frozen foods and reheating leftovers.

Microwave cooking is not magic. It doesn't cook everything more quickly than other methods, nor is it always more convenient. But there are foods that microwave ovens cook better, faster or more efficiently and these are the focus of this book.

Campbell's family of products teams up with your microwave oven to help you make the most of every minute you spend in the kitchen. The rich, full flavours of Campbell's Soups, Broths, Prego Spaghetti Sauces and Franco-American Gravies put homemade taste into your quick meals. Swanson Frozen Dinners and Entrées and Le Menu Dinners help you skip major cooking steps. Pepperidge Farm products and V8 Vegetable Juice work as both recipe ingredients and accompaniments to fine meals.

There is one message we'd most like you to take away from this book: *Microwave cooking is simply another way to cook.* Your microwave oven will never replace all your other cooking appliances, but, as you gain experience, you'll discover it's the best appliance for many cooking steps and a great friend to busy people.

We asked a panel of experienced microwave oven owners what advice they would like to pass on to others. Their advice was the same as ours: *Use it!* The more you do the more you'll learn about the benefits of microwave cooking.

We hope this book will help you do just that.

How Your Microwave Oven Works

Inside your microwave oven is a magnetron tube that converts electrical energy into microwave energy. The microwave energy is directed into the oven and reflects off the walls and floor until it is absorbed by the food, making the food hot. Because microwaves work directly on the food, they don't waste energy heating the air or the food's container. That's why microwaves heat many foods more quickly and efficiently than other cooking methods do.

If you've ever used a microwave oven other than your own, you know how different they can be—with different controls on the outside, larger or smaller cavities, maybe a shelf or a turntable inside.

Microwave ovens also vary greatly in how they work. Some have energy entering the oven from the top, some from the bottom, some from the sides and some from more than one direction. Some cook more quickly, some more slowly; some heat more evenly, while others have "hot spots" where food tends to cook first.

To learn how to use your appliance, read the manual that came with it, then experiment with a variety of foods. You'll learn where the hot spots are in your oven and whether it consistently cooks foods more slowly or more quickly than average.

What Microwave Ovens Do Best

Because the results of microwave cooking are similar to those of steam cooking, the microwave oven works best on foods you might otherwise steam. High-moisture foods such as vegetables and fruits are naturals, as are tender fish and chicken. Meats that benefit from the moist heat of braising also work well.

Cakes and breads can be cooked in the microwave oven; however, the results may disappoint you because the short cooking time and moist heat will not produce conventional oven texture and browning.

Foods that require rehydrating, such as rice, pasta and dried beans, can be microwaved, but will require the same amount of cooking time as conventional cooking. Because these foods have a tendency to boil over in the microwave oven, you may prefer to cook them conventionally.

Foods that should have a crisp, brown crust do not work well in the microwave oven without special equipment. Very large quantities of liquid may require more time in the microwave oven than on the stove. Deep-fat frying should not be attempted in the microwave oven.

Factors That Affect Microwave Cooking

Don't get the idea that you must forget everything you know about cooking. Microwave cooking isn't really so different from traditional cooking, and the factors that affect microwave cooking time are similar to those that affect any cooking method.

For example, microwave cooking is greatly affected by the **quantity** of food in the oven. In your microwave oven, 250 mL (1 cup) of water boils nearly twice as fast as 500 mL (2 cups). The same is true of water in a kettle on the stove. This means additional time is needed for the added potato or onion in a recipe or the extra-large chicken breast you bought.

The **size** of food pieces also affects the cooking time. Small cubes of potato cook more quickly and evenly than larger ones. Thin slices cook more quickly than thicker ones.

Appropriate **arrangement** of the food in your microwave oven can help the food cook better. Arrangements with thicker, slower-cooking pieces toward the outside edge usually work best. The food in the centre is generally the last to cook. The same principle applies to **shapes** of foods such as cakes and casseroles. Round or ring shapes work best; corners of square foods may cook too quickly.

Variations in the **starting temperature of a food** can change its cooking time. You know the same is true of conventional cooking, if you've ever tried to cook a frozen roast. However, shorter microwave cooking times make the difference more apparent.

The **composition of a food** can affect the way it heats. Foods with higher concentrations of fat, sugar or salt attract microwaves more readily than those with lower concentrations.

Using the **proper utensil** makes a difference too. Be sure to use a dish large enough to allow for boiling and stirring. Consider how full you'd want a saucepan, not an oven-going casserole. Food tends to cook more evenly in round dishes rather than those with corners. Food spread out in a shallow dish will cook faster than the same food placed in a deep, narrow dish.

Microwave ovens vary (by manufacturer, model and even by unit) in how quickly and evenly they cook. Your microwave oven may have a **wave pattern** that requires you to stir or rotate foods more often than recipes suggest, or it may cook so evenly that you can skip some of these directions. Experience with your oven can teach you that.

In some microwave ovens, **elevating** the food on an inverted microwave-safe pie plate may bring it into a more favourable wave pattern, especially for baked goods and quiches.

Wattage

One thing you should know about your microwave oven is its **wattage**. Wattage is a good indicator of how fast your oven will cook. The recipes have been tested in 650- and 700-watt microwave ovens. These are among the fastest cooking microwave ovens. Many of the smaller units being sold today are rated lower—as low as 350 watts—and therefore cook more slowly. If you have one of these, you will need to add more time to each step of every recipe.

The actual wattage output of your microwave oven may vary with other conditions too. For example, when electrical demand is high (as in the summer when air conditioners are operating), voltage entering the house may be lower than normal, causing your microwave oven to operate less efficiently. Even operating several appliances at once in your own home can decrease efficiency.

You may find the wattage rating for your microwave oven listed in the use-and-care guide, or it may be printed somewhere on the appliance. If you can't find it, you can perform a simple test to approximate the wattage (see box below) or contact the manufacturer.

Wattage Test

This quick test will give you an idea of the wattage output of your microwave oven.

Combine 250 mL (1 cup) of water with ice in a 500 mL (2 cup) measure. Stir 2 min or until ice stops melting and water is very cold. Remove ice; pour 250 mL (1 cup) of the cold water into a 250 mL (1 cup) glass measure. Microwave, uncovered, on HIGH until water begins to boil.

If water boils in less than 3.5 min, your microwave oven is producing 600 to 700 watts of energy on HIGH. If it takes 3.5 to 4.5 min to boil, wattage output is 500 to 600 watts. If the heating time is longer than 4.5 min, the wattage output is less than 500 watts.

This test will give you an approximate idea of wattage output. However, your microwave oven's efficiency may vary depending on the quantity and kind of food being cooked.

Microwave Cooking Know-How

To use your microwave oven most effectively, you should be familiar with some pointers that will make these and other microwave recipes the best they can be.

Power Setting

Most of today's microwave ovens have a range of power settings to choose from, and they vary from oven to oven, even within the same brand. Settings may have names such as "defrost", "simmer" or "medium" or they may be indicated by numbers from one to ten. For power settings other than HIGH, the microwave power cycles on and off, controlling the total amount of microwave energy being sent to the food. Higher power settings are used for faster cooking while lower settings help to cook food more slowly and evenly.

Two different power settings are used in these recipes. **HIGH** power is called for most often. On HIGH, the microwave oven is operating at full power the entire time it is on. At **50% POWER** the microwave energy cycles on and off at equal intervals to provide slower cooking. Your oven may have other names for these settings, so consult your use-and-care manual or contact the manufacturer for more information.

If your microwave oven has a low wattage rating, you may wish to compensate for the lower wattage by using a higher setting, such as 60% or 70%, when we call for 50% power.

Containers

You probably know that metal cooking containers are rarely used in the microwave oven because they reflect waves away from the food, slowing the cooking. Metal, if improperly used, may also cause arcing (sparks). The metallic gold or silver trim on some china may arc and discolour, so these dishes should also be avoided. Your microwave oven manual will explain what, if any, metal may be used in your particular oven. If you do use metal, be sure to use only small amounts and to keep it away from the sides and floor of the oven, which may be metal.

There are many glass and ceramic utensils available on the market today made especially for microwave cooking, but not all kinds of glassware and china are suitable for microwave oven use. To test whether a container is microwavable, place it in your microwave oven alongside a cup of cold water. Microwave on HIGH 1 min. If the water is warm and the container is cool, the container may be used. If the container is warm or has warm spots, it is not microwavable. (This test is not suitable for plastic containers.)

Many plastics are ideal for microwave cooking, and today's stores are full of plastics that have been developed especially for microwave oven use. There are other plastics that are unsuitable for microwaving—some because they can melt from the heat of the food, others because they absorb microwaves. To be certain, use only plastics that the manufacturer says are microwave-safe.

Paper plates and paper towels may be used for some microwave cooking. Avoid using paper towels with dyes that may leach into the food. Recycled paper products are not recommended because they contain materials that could ignite in your microwave oven.

There are some specialty items you may wish to buy for microwave cooking. For example, browning trays can give meats a browned appearance and flavour, microwave meat racks hold bacon and other meats above their drippings, and some microwave muffin pans have perforated bottoms that allow steam to escape.

How to Tell the Size of a Casserole or Baking Dish

If you're not sure how much your casseroles hold, there's a simple way to determine their volume. Simply fill the dish with a measured amount of water. The quantity of water needed to fill the dish to the rim is its volume.

For baking dishes, the measurements given are for the dish's length and width, measured from the inside edges.

Covers

Covering a food holds in steam to keep it moist, distributes the heat more evenly and contains spatters.

Close-fitting lids and **plastic wrap** can be used interchangeably for the tightest covers. Choose a lid that is made of a microwave-safe material that fits the dish snugly.

Plastic wrap is especially versatile because it will fit any size or shape of dish. Look for a brand that claims to be microwavable; some others may melt if they touch hot food. When you use plastic wrap, fold back one corner of the wrap to provide a vent for the excess steam to escape, or the wrap may split.

Always remove a tight cover carefully, away from your face; even though the dish may seem cool, steam built up under the cover may be very hot and dangerous.

When you want to keep a minimum of steam in the dish, cover the food loosely with **waxed paper** to keep the food moist and control spatters. A paper towel cover can absorb grease or excess moisture; again, use **paper towels** that are free of dyes and have not been made from recycled paper products.

Some foods, such as cakes and foods with a crumb coating, are cooked uncovered to promote a dry, not soggy surface.

Stirring, Rotating and Rearranging

To cook food more evenly, recipes often call for stirring, rotating or rearranging the food. **Stirring** is most effective in distributing the heat; just stir the food with a spoon to distribute the heat throughout the dish.

Foods that cannot be stirred, such as fish and layered casseroles, should be **rotated**. Rotate a dish by turning it in a counterclockwise or clockwise motion; one-quarter (90°) turns are most effective, but one half (180°) turns can be used when a dish is longer than the oven is wide. If your microwave oven has a turntable, you will not need to rotate the dish.

Rearrange when there are several pieces of food or dishes in the oven. When rearranging, turn foods so that they are in a different position in the oven and the outside pieces are toward the inside. If possible, turn foods over so that bottoms are on top.

Doneness and Standing Time

Some recipes call for standing time to complete cooking and to allow heat to distribute evenly throughout the food. For standing, simply place the food directly on a flat surface such as a countertop or cutting board. Better yet; leave the dish in the microwave oven with the power off. Do not use a cooling rack.

It is easy to overcook foods in a microwave oven, so if the food seems nearly done, let it stand, then check for doneness, adding more cooking time in short intervals as needed.

Modifying Microwave Recipes

You may be so used to doubling or halving conventional recipes that you don't think about it. Microwave recipes need more consideration.

When doubling a microwave recipe, be sure the dish size is adequate. You may not want to double the liquid, because evaporation is slower than in conventional cooking. You'll definitely need more cooking time; start with about 50% more time, then check for doneness.

When you halve a recipe, keep the same size dish, but reduce the cooking time. Start with half of the cooking time of the full recipe, checking often for doneness.

If you alter a recipe, you can affect the cooking time. See *Factors That Affect Microwave Cooking* on page 6 for more information.

Microwave Cooking Times

Cooking times for recipes depend on your oven wattage and other factors. The recipe time given in this book are *the minimum cooking times* needed in 650- to 700-watt ovens. Your oven may consistently require more time than suggested, especially if you have a 400- to 500-watt oven. (See page 8 for more information on wattage.) For the best indicator of cooking time, follow the recipe descriptions of how the food should look when done.

Caring for Your Microwave Oven

Your microwave oven needs some care. Keep it clean and do not obstruct any vents. Place it on a stable surface where it will not be jarred.

For best results, plug your oven into its own grounded circuit. Be aware that anytime several appliances are on the same electrical circuit, the combination may overload the circuit.

Never operate your microwave oven when empty. If you have children who may turn it on, keep a cup of water inside to absorb microwaves.

Microwave ovens are very safe. However, if yours has been damaged in some way, microwave leakage may occur. In such a case, have it checked by a microwave service professional.

Campbell Microwave Institute

The Campbell Microwave Institute (CMI) was established in 1986 to promote microwave cooking, both by improving the quality of microwavable foods and by teaching consumers to make the most of their microwave ovens. It's a big task, but one that our team of scientists, home economists and other specialists is well-qualified to tackle.

This book fulfills a small part of our mission. It will help take the mystery out of microwave cooking for you and show you how to use your microwave oven in many different ways every day.

In other areas of consumer education and product development, CMI has already made outstanding progress. Here are a few examples of our work:

- Swanson Dinners and Entrées and Le Menu Dinners are now packaged in microwavable plastic or paperboard containers.
- Microwave cooking directions are included on most of our packaging including Campbell's Soups, Franco-American Gravies and Prego Spaghetti Sauces, as well as the frozen foods mentioned above.
- We've developed award-winning microwavable packaging in our recently opened Campbell Plastics Centre, packages that will simplify your daily cooking chores and improve the results of foods prepared in the microwave oven.
- We've worked on research to further the scientific knowledge of how food and packaging materials respond to microwave energy, and have shared our findings with the microwave industry and media representatives.
- We've made our team of experts available to newspapers, magazines, and other news media to keep them abreast of the latest developments in this fast-changing subject area, so they can transmit this information to you.

Whether you're a microwave cooking novice or a pro, there is much to learn. Let us know if you have any insights to share or questions we can answer and we will continue to be the microwave cooking resource that meets the needs of home cooks and professionals.

Soups

Golden Broccoli Soup

500 mL	**broccoli flowerets**	**2 cups**
125 mL	**grated carrot**	**½ cup**
125 mL	**chopped onion**	**½ cup**
50 mL	**water**	**¼ cup**
284 mL	**can Campbell's Condensed Cream of Potato Soup**	**10 ounce**
1	**soup can milk**	**1**
250 mL	**grated Cheddar cheese**	**1 cup**
1 mL	**pepper**	**¼ teaspoon**

1. In 3 L (3 quart) microwave-safe casserole, combine broccoli, carrot, onion and water. Cover with lid; microwave on HIGH 5 min or until vegetables are tender.

2. In small bowl, stir soup until smooth. Stir in remaining ingredients. Stir into vegetables. Cover; microwave on HIGH 8 min or until hot and bubbling, stirring twice during cooking. Let stand, covered, 5 min before serving. Makes 1 L (4 cups) or 4 servings.

GOLDEN BROCCOLI SOUP ▶

Upper Canada Pumpkin Soup

50 mL	finely chopped onion	¼ cup
25 mL	butter or margarine	2 tablespoons
284 mL	can Campbell's Condensed Cream of Chicken or Cream of Mushroom Soup	10 ounce
250 mL	canned or mashed cooked pumpkin	1 cup
Dash	ground nutmeg	Dash
Dash	pepper	Dash
	Chopped fresh parsley for garnish	

1. In 2 L (2 quart) microwave-safe casserole, combine onion and butter. Cover with lid; microwave on HIGH 2 min or until onion is tender.

2. In medium bowl, combine remaining ingredients; stir into casserole. Cover; microwave on HIGH 5 min or until hot and bubbling, stirring once during cooking.

3. Garnish with parsley before serving if desired. Makes about 750 mL (3 cups) or 3 servings.

Cucumber-Leek Soup

2 (284 mL)	cans Campbell's Condensed Chicken Broth	2 (10 ounce)
125 mL	water	½ cup
1	large cucumber, peeled, seeded and sliced	1
1	large leek, sliced (white part only)	1
25 mL	chopped fresh parsley	2 tablespoons
2 mL	dried dill weed, crushed	½ teaspoon
Dash	pepper	Dash
50 mL	plain yogurt	¼ cup

1. In 2 L (2 quart) microwave-safe casserole, combine broth, water, cucumber and leek. Cover with lid; microwave on HIGH 8 min or until boiling.

2. With slotted spoon, transfer vegetables to blender or food processor. Add 125 mL (½ cup) of the broth mixture, parsley, dill and pepper. Cover; blend until smooth. Return mixture to broth. Cover; microwave on HIGH 4 min or until hot and bubbling.

3. Ladle soup into bowls; top with yogurt and additional dill weed if desired. Makes about 1 L (4 cups) or 4 servings.

UPPER CANADA PUMPKIN SOUP ▶

Curried Zucchini Soup

For an elegant presentation, serve bowls of chilled soup in liners packed with crushed ice.

15 mL	**butter or margarine**	**1 tablespoon**
500 mL	**coarsely chopped zucchini**	**2 cups**
25 mL	**chopped green onion**	**2 tablespoons**
5 mL	**curry powder**	**1 teaspoon**
284 mL	**can Campbell's Condensed Cream of Potato Soup**	**10 ounce**
450 mL	**milk**	**1¾ cups**
	Croûtons for garnish	

1. In 2 L (2 quart) microwave-safe casserole, combine butter, zucchini, onion and curry powder. Cover with lid; microwave on HIGH 7 min or until zucchini is very tender, stirring once during cooking.

2. Stir soup into zucchini mixture. In covered blender or food processor, blend soup mixture until smooth. Return to casserole. Stir in milk.

3. Cover; refrigerate until serving time, at least 4 h. Thin chilled soup to desired consistency with additional milk. Ladle into bowls. Garnish with croûtons. Makes about 1 L (4 cups) or 4 servings.

NOTE: To serve this soup hot, prepare as above through step 2. Cover; microwave on HIGH 4 min or until hot and bubbling.

Fresh Spinach Soup

15 mL	**butter or margarine**	**1 tablespoon**
500 mL	**loosely packed chopped spinach leaves**	**2 cups**
284 mL	**can Campbell's Condensed Cream of Potato Soup**	**10 ounce**
1	**soup can milk**	**1**
25 mL	**dry sherry or vermouth**	**2 tablespoons**
Dash	**ground nutmeg**	**Dash**

1. In 2 L (2 quart) microwave-safe casserole, combine butter and spinach. Cover with lid; microwave on HIGH 2 min or until spinach is wilted.

2. Stir in soup until smooth; stir in remaining ingredients. Cover; microwave on HIGH 6 min or until hot and bubbling, stirring once during cooking. Makes about 750 mL (3 cups) or 3 servings.

CURRIED ZUCCHINI SOUP ▶

Apple Cheese Soup

This soup is delicious served hot or cold.

2	**apples, peeled, cored and chopped**	**2**
15 mL	**water**	**1 tablespoon**
1 mL	**ground nutmeg**	**¼ teaspoon**
1 mL	**ground cinnamon**	**¼ teaspoon**
284 mL	**can Campbell's Condensed Cheddar Cheese Soup**	**10 ounce**
200 mL	**milk**	**¾ cup**
	Sour cream or plain yogurt for garnish	

1. In 2 L (2 quart) microwave-safe casserole, combine apples, water, nutmeg and cinnamon. Cover with lid; microwave on HIGH 5 min or until apples are very tender, stirring once during cooking.

2. Stir soup into apple mixture. In covered blender or food processor, blend soup mixture until smooth. Return to casserole. Stir in milk. Cover; microwave on HIGH 3 min or until hot and bubbling. Garnish with sour cream and additional nutmeg if desired. Makes about 750 mL (3 cups) or 3 servings.

Double Onion Soup Gratinée

Easier to eat and easier to use than traditional French bread slices, croûtons also add more flavour to this updated soup.

15 mL	**butter or margarine**	**1 tablespoon**
2	**green onions, thinly sliced**	**2**
284 mL	**can Campbell's Condensed Onion Soup**	**10 ounce**
1	**soup can water**	**1**
25 mL	**dry vermouth**	**2 tablespoons**
250 mL	**seasoned croûtons**	**1 cup**
250 mL	**grated Swiss cheese**	**1 cup**

1. In 1 L (4 cup) glass measure, combine butter and onions. Microwave, uncovered, on HIGH 1 min or until onions are wilted.

2. Stir in soup, water and vermouth. Microwave, uncovered, on HIGH 5 min or until boiling, stirring once during cooking.

3. Ladle soup into 3 bowls. Sprinkle croûtons over soup; sprinkle with cheese. Let stand, uncovered, 1 min or until cheese is melted. Makes about 750 mL (3 cups) or 3 servings.

Chilled Cream of Parsley Soup

15 mL	**butter or margarine**	**1 tablespoon**
375 mL	**finely chopped fresh parsley**	**1½ cups**
284 mL	**can Campbell's Condensed Cream of Celery Soup**	**10 ounce**
1	**soup can milk**	**1**
1	**egg yolk**	**1**
15 mL	**lemon juice**	**1 tablespoon**
Dash	**cayenne pepper**	**Dash**
125 mL	**heavy cream, whipped**	**½ cup**

1. In 2 L (2 quart) microwave-safe casserole, combine butter and parsley. Cover with lid; microwave on HIGH 3 min or until parsley is wilted.

2. Stir in soup until smooth; stir in milk. Cover; microwave on HIGH 7 min or until boiling.

3. In small bowl, beat egg yolk. Slowly beat 125 mL (½ cup) hot soup mixture into yolk. Return egg mixture to soup. Stir in lemon juice and cayenne pepper. Carefully pour into blender or food processor. Cover; blend until smooth.

4. Return mixture to casserole. Cover; refrigerate until serving time, at least 4 h. Garnish with whipped cream and additional parsley if desired. Makes about 750 mL (3 cups) or 3 servings.

Pasta and Cheese Soup

284 mL	**can Campbell's Condensed Tomato Soup**	**10 ounce**
284 mL	**can Campbell's Condensed Cheddar Cheese Soup**	**10 ounce**
2	**soup cans milk**	**2**
375 mL	**sliced zucchini**	**1½ cups**
125 mL	**sweet red pepper, cut into 2.5 cm (1 inch) squares**	**½ cup**
5 mL	**dried oregano leaves, crushed**	**1 teaspoon**
1 mL	**garlic powder**	**¼ teaspoon**
375 mL	**cooked corkscrew macaroni**	**1½ cups**

1. In 3 L (3 quart) microwave-safe casserole, stir soups well. Gradually stir in milk. Add zucchini, pepper, oregano and garlic powder.

2. Cover with lid; microwave on HIGH 12 min or until zucchini is tender, stirring twice during cooking. Add macaroni. Cover; microwave on HIGH 3 min or until hot. Makes about 1.75 L (7 cups) or 7 servings.

Oriental Vegetable Soup

284 mL	can Campbell's Condensed Chicken Broth	10 ounce
1	soup can water	1
15 mL	soy sauce	1 tablespoon
15 mL	dry sherry	1 tablespoon
Dash	ground ginger	Dash
125 mL	frozen cut green beans	½ cup
50 mL	thinly sliced carrot	¼ cup
50 mL	cubed tofu	¼ cup

1. In 2 L (2 quart) microwave-safe casserole, combine broth, water, soy sauce, sherry and ginger. Stir in beans and carrot. Cover with lid; microwave on HIGH 10 min or until soup is boiling and vegetables are tender-crisp.

2. Stir in tofu. Let stand, covered, 2 min. Makes about 1.25 L (5 cups) or 5 servings.

NOTE: To make carrot flowers: Use an hors d'oeuvre cutter or sharp knife to cut carrot slices into flower shapes. For easier cutting, microwave whole carrot on HIGH 1 min or until slightly softened.

Egg Drop Soup

284 mL	can Campbell's Condensed Chicken Broth	10 ounce
1	soup can water	1
15 mL	cornstarch	1 tablespoon
15 mL	rice wine vinegar or dry sherry	1 tablespoon
10 mL	soy sauce	2 teaspoons
125 mL	cooked ham cut into thin strips	½ cup
125 mL	snow peas	½ cup
3	green onions, sliced	3
2	eggs, beaten	2

1. In 2 L (2 quart) microwave-safe casserole, stir together broth, water, cornstarch, vinegar and soy sauce. Stir in ham, snow peas, and onions. Cover with lid; microwave on HIGH 10 min or until boiling, stirring twice during cooking.

2. With fork, stir broth with a swirling motion. Without stirring, slowly pour eggs into swirling broth, then stir just until eggs are set in long strands. Makes about 1 L (4 cups) or 4 servings.

ORIENTAL VEGETABLE SOUP ▶

Creamy Fish Chowder

4	slices bacon, chopped	4
250 mL	thinly sliced carrots	1 cup
125 mL	chopped onion	½ cup
284 mL	can Campbell's Condensed Cream of Potato Soup	10 ounce
375 mL	milk	1½ cups
250 g	firm, white fish, cut into pieces	½ pound
25 mL	chopped fresh parsley	2 tablespoons

1. Place bacon in 2 L (2 quart) microwave-safe casserole. Cover with paper towel; microwave on HIGH 3 min or until crisp, stirring once during cooking. Transfer bacon to paper towels, reserving drippings in casserole.

2. Add carrots and onion to bacon drippings. Cover with lid; microwave on HIGH 4 min or until vegetables are tender, stirring once during cooking.

3. Stir in remaining ingredients; mix well. Cover; microwave on HIGH 9 min or until fish is opaque and flakes easily when tested with fork, stirring once during cooking. Garnish with reserved bacon. Makes about 1 L (4 cups) or 4 servings.

Hearty Borscht

25 mL	butter or margarine	2 tablespoons
125 mL	chopped onion	½ cup
455 mL	can whole beets, drained and coarsely chopped	16 ounce
500 mL	coarsely chopped cabbage	2 cups
284 mL	can Campbell's Home Cookin' Old Fashioned Vegetable Beef Soup	10 ounce
284 mL	can Campbell's Condensed Beef Broth	10 ounce
250 mL	water	1 cup
15 mL	lemon juice	1 tablespoon
5 mL	sugar	1 teaspoon
1 mL	pepper	¼ teaspoon
125 mL	sour cream for garnish	½ cup
25 mL	chopped chives or green onions for garnish	2 tablespoons

1. In 3 L (3 quart) microwave-safe casserole, combine butter and onion. Cover with lid; microwave on HIGH 3 min or until tender, stirring once during cooking.

2. Stir in beets, cabbage, soup, broth, water, lemon juice, sugar and pepper. Cover; microwave on HIGH 12 min or until boiling, stirring once during cooking. Let stand, covered, 5 min.

3. In small bowl, mix sour cream and chives. Ladle soup into bowls. Garnish with sour cream mixture. Makes about 1.5 L (6 cups) or 6 servings.

Clam Tomato Soup

18	**small clams with shells**	**18**
15 mL	**olive oil**	**1 tablespoon**
125 mL	**sliced celery**	**½ cup**
125 mL	**green pepper, cut into 5 cm (2 inch) strips**	**½ cup**
1	**large clove garlic, minced**	**1**
2 mL	**dried thyme leaves, crushed**	**½ teaspoon**
284 mL	**can Campbell's Condensed Tomato Soup**	**10 ounce**
1	**soup can water**	**1**
50 mL	**Chablis or other dry white wine**	**¼ cup**
Dash	**hot pepper sauce**	**Dash**
175 mL	**cooked rice**	**⅔ cup**

1. Discard any clams that do not start to close when lightly tapped. Scrub clams under cold running water.

2. In 3 L (3 quart) microwave-safe casserole, combine oil, celery, green pepper, garlic and thyme. Cover with lid; microwave on HIGH 2.5 min or until tender, stirring once during cooking.

3. Stir in soup, water, Chablis, hot pepper sauce and clams. Cover; microwave at 50% power 12 min or until shells open. Discard any unopened clams.

4. Stir in rice. Cover; microwave at 50% power 2 min or until hot. Makes about 1 L (4 cups) or 4 servings.

Avocado Tomato Soup

15 mL	**butter or margarine**	**1 tablespoon**
50 mL	**thinly sliced celery**	**¼ cup**
2 mL	**chili powder**	**½ teaspoon**
Dash	**ground cinnamon**	**Dash**
284 mL	**can Campbell's Condensed Tomato Soup**	**10 ounce**
1	**soup can water**	**1**
10 mL	**lemon juice**	**2 teaspoons**
125 mL	**chopped avocado**	**½ cup**

1. In 1.5 L (1½ quart) microwave-safe casserole, combine butter, celery, chili powder and cinnamon. Cover with lid; microwave on HIGH 3 min or until celery is tender, stirring once during cooking.

2. Stir in soup, water and lemon juice. Cover; microwave on HIGH 3 min or until hot and bubbling. Stir in avocado. Makes about 750 mL (3 cups) or 3 servings.

Bavarian Pea Soup

15 mL	**butter or margarine**	**1 tablespoon**
125 mL	**shredded cabbage**	**½ cup**
1 mL	**caraway seed**	**¼ teaspoon**
540 mL	**can Campbell's Home Cookin' Split Pea with Ham Soup**	**19 ounce**
	Dark rye bread, torn into pieces	
	Grated Swiss cheese	

1. In 1 L (1 quart) microwave-safe casserole, combine butter, cabbage and caraway. Cover with lid; microwave on HIGH 3 min or until cabbage is tender, stirring once during cooking.

2. Stir in soup. Cover; microwave on HIGH 4 min or until heated through, stirring once during cooking.

3. Pour soup into 2 microwave-safe soup bowls; top with bread and cheese. Microwave, uncovered, on HIGH 1 min or until cheese is melted. Makes 500 mL (2 cups) or 2 servings.

Dutch Chowder

375 mL	**cooked chicken, cut into strips**	**1½ cups**
50 mL	**chopped onion**	**¼ cup**
25 mL	**butter or margarine**	**2 tablespoons**
2 (284 mL)	**cans Campbell's Condensed Pea Soup**	**2 (10 ounce)**
1.5	**soup cans water**	**1½**
284 g	**package frozen mixed vegetables, cooked and drained**	**10 ounce**
1 mL	**ground nutmeg**	**¼ teaspoon**

1. In 3 L (3 quart) microwave-safe casserole, combine chicken, onion and butter. Cover with lid; microwave on HIGH 4 min, stirring once during cooking.

2. Stir in soup; gradually blend in water. Stir in remaining ingredients. Cover; microwave on HIGH 5 min or until hot and bubbling, stirring twice during cooking. Makes 1.75 L (7 cups) or 6 servings.

BAVARIAN PEA SOUP ▶

Curried Broccoli Chicken Soup

500 mL	**chopped broccoli**	**2 cups**
	OR	
284 g	**package frozen chopped broccoli, thawed and drained**	**10 ounce**
125 mL	**chopped onion**	**½ cup**
15 mL	**butter or margarine**	**1 tablespoon**
5 mL	**curry powder**	**1 teaspoon**
284 mL	**can Campbell's Condensed Cream of Chicken Soup**	**10 ounce**
1	**soup can milk**	**1**
125 mL	**diced cooked chicken or turkey**	**½ cup**

1. In 2 L (2 quart) microwave-safe casserole, combine broccoli, onion, butter and curry powder. Cover with lid; microwave on HIGH 5 min or until broccoli is tender-crisp, stirring occasionally.

2. Stir in soup and milk. Cover; microwave on HIGH 5 min or until hot, stirring occasionally. Stir in chicken. Let stand, covered, 2 min before serving. Makes about 750 mL (3 cups) or 3 servings.

Greek Lemon Soup

Orzo is a small rice-shaped pasta that is traditional in this classic Greek soup.

284 mL	**can Campbell's Condensed Chicken Broth**	**10 ounce**
1	**soup can water**	**1**
50 mL	**orzo or regular long-grain rice, uncooked**	**¼ cup**
2	**eggs**	**2**
25 mL	**lemon juice**	**2 tablespoons**
	Thin lemon slices for garnish	

1. In 2 L (2 quart) microwave-safe casserole, combine broth, water and orzo. Cover with lid; microwave on HIGH 8 min or until boiling. Stir soup.

2. Reduce power to 50%. Cover; microwave 18 min or until orzo is tender, stirring once during cooking.

3. In small bowl, beat eggs and lemon juice. Slowly beat 125 mL (½ cup) hot soup into egg mixture. Return egg mixture to broth, stirring constantly until soup is slightly thickened. Garnish with lemon slices. Makes about 1 L (4 cups) or 4 servings.

Chicken-Corn Soup

15 mL	**butter or margarine**	**1 tablespoon**
1	**clove garlic, minced**	**1**
284 mL	**can Campbell's Condensed Chicken Broth**	**10**
1	**soup can water**	**1**
398 g	**can cream-style corn**	**14 ounce**
250 mL	**diced cooked chicken**	**1 cup**
2 mL	**finely chopped hot peppers**	**½ teaspoon**
1 mL	**ground cumin**	**¼ teaspoon**
	Tortilla chips	

1. In 2 L (2 quart) microwave-safe casserole, combine butter and garlic. Cover with lid; microwave on HIGH 30 sec or until butter is melted.

2. Stir in broth, water, corn, chicken, peppers and cumin. Cover; microwave on HIGH 5 min or until hot and bubbling. Place a few tortilla chips in the bottom of each of 4 soup bowls. Ladle hot soup over chips. Makes about 1 L (4 cups) or 4 servings.

Lemony Chicken Soup

15 mL	**butter or margarine**	**1 tablespoon**
125 mL	**carrots, cut into julienne strips**	**½ cup**
125 mL	**sliced fresh mushrooms**	**½ cup**
25 mL	**sliced green onion**	**2 tablespoons**
284 mL	**can Campbell's Condensed Chicken Noodle Soup**	**10 ounce**
1	**soup can water**	**1**
5 mL	**lemon juice**	**1 teaspoon**
Dash	**white pepper**	**Dash**
	Chopped fresh parsley	

1. In 2 L (2 quart) microwave-safe casserole, combine butter, carrots, mushrooms and onion. Cover with lid; microwave on HIGH 3 min or until vegetables are tender-crisp, stirring once during cooking.

2. Stir in soup, water, lemon juice and pepper. Cover; microwave on HIGH 4 min or until hot and bubbling, stirring twice during cooking. Garnish with parsley. Makes about 750 mL (3 cups) or 3 servings.

Poultry

Country Captain

1.25 kg	**chicken parts, skinned**	**2½ pounds**
284 mL	**can Campbell's Condensed Tomato Soup**	**10 ounce**
1	**green pepper, cut into 1.5 cm (½ inch) pieces**	**1**
50 mL	**raisins**	**¼ cup**
5 mL	**curry powder**	**1 teaspoon**
50 mL	**toasted slivered almonds (see Note on page 98)**	**¼ cup**
	Hot cooked rice	

1. Arrange chicken in 30 by 20 cm (12 by 8 inch) microwave-safe baking dish, placing thicker portions toward edges of dish.

2. In small bowl, combine soup, pepper, raisins and curry powder; spoon over chicken.

3. Cover with waxed paper; microwave on HIGH 22 min or until chicken is no longer pink in centre, rearranging chicken and basting with pan juices once during cooking. Let stand, covered, 5 min. Sprinkle with almonds. Serve over rice. Makes 6 servings.

COUNTRY CAPTAIN ▶

Italian Chicken

1.25 kg	**chicken parts, skinned**	**2½ pounds**
250 mL	**sliced fresh mushrooms**	**1 cup**
125 mL	**chopped onion**	**½ cup**
450 mL	**Prego Spaghetti Sauce**	**1¾ cups**

1. Arrange chicken in 30 by 20 cm (12 by 8 inch) microwave-safe baking dish, placing thicker portions toward edges of dish. Top with mushrooms and onion. Pour spaghetti sauce over chicken.

2. Cover with waxed paper; microwave on HIGH 22 min or until chicken is no longer pink in centre, rearranging chicken once during cooking. Let stand, covered, 5 min. Makes 6 servings.

Arroz Con Pollo

15 mL	**olive or vegetable oil**	**1 tablespoon**
1	**clove garlic, minced**	**1**
284 mL	**can Campbell's Condensed Chicken Broth**	**10 ounce**
398 mL	**can tomatoes, undrained, cut up**	**14 ounce**
250 mL	**regular long-grain rice, uncooked**	**1 cup**
Dash	**ground turmeric**	**Dash**
1 kg	**chicken thighs, skinned**	**2 pounds**
250 mL	**frozen peas**	**1 cup**

1. In 30 by 20 cm (12 by 8 inch) microwave-safe baking dish, combine oil and garlic. Cover with vented plastic wrap; microwave on HIGH 1 min.

2. Stir in broth and tomatoes with their liquid. Cover; microwave on HIGH 5 min or until boiling.

3. Stir in rice and turmeric. Arrange chicken over rice, placing thicker portions toward edges of dish. Cover; microwave on HIGH 8 min.

4. Remove chicken. Stir peas into rice; rearrange chicken over rice. Cover; microwave on HIGH 15 min or until rice is nearly done and chicken is no longer pink in centre, rotating dish once during cooking. Let stand, covered, 10 min or until rice is tender. Makes 6 servings.

Glorified Chicken

1.25 kg	**chicken parts, skinned**	**2½ pounds**
284 mL	**can Campbell's Condensed Cream of Chicken or Cream of Mushroom Soup**	**10 ounce**
25 mL	**chopped fresh parsley**	**2 tablespoons**

1. Arrange chicken in 30 by 20 cm (12 by 8 inch) microwave-safe baking dish, placing thicker portions toward edges of dish.

2. In small bowl, stir soup until smooth; stir in parsley. Spread soup evenly over chicken.

3. Cover with waxed paper; microwave on HIGH 20 min or until chicken is no longer pink in centre, rearranging chicken and basting with pan juices once during cooking. Let stand, covered, 5 min. Makes 6 servings.

Herbed Chicken with Potatoes

25 mL	**butter or margarine**	**2 tablespoons**
500 g	**potatoes, peeled and cubed**	**1 pound**
284 mL	**can Campbell's Condensed Cream of Chicken Soup**	**10 ounce**
25 mL	**dry sherry**	**2 tablespoons**
15 mL	**orange juice**	**1 tablespoon**
1 mL	**rubbed sage**	**¼ teaspoon**
4	**skinless boneless chicken breast halves**	**4**
	Orange slices for garnish	

1. In 3 L (3 quart) microwave-safe casserole, combine butter and potatoes. Cover with lid; microwave on HIGH 5 min or until potatoes are almost tender, stirring once during cooking.

2. In small bowl, stir soup until smooth; stir in sherry, orange juice and sage.

3. Arrange chicken in circular pattern over potatoes. Pour soup mixture over chicken. Cover; microwave on HIGH 15 min or until chicken is no longer pink in centre, rotating dish once during cooking. Let stand, covered, 5 min. Garnish with orange slices. Makes 4 servings.

Rolled Chicken Breasts Florentine

4	**skinless boneless chicken breast halves**	**4**
4	**thin slices cooked ham**	**4**
4	**thin slices Swiss cheese**	**4**
284 g	**package frozen chopped spinach, thawed and well drained (see Note below)**	**10 ounce**
284 mL	**can Campbell's Condensed Cream of Chicken or Cream of Mushroom Soup**	**10 ounce**
75 mL	**water**	**⅓ cup**
50 mL	**sliced green onions**	**¼ cup**
Dash	**dried thyme leaves, crushed**	**Dash**

1. With flat side of meat mallet, pound chicken to 1 cm (¼ inch) thickness. Place 1 ham slice, 1 cheese slice and ¼ of the spinach on each chicken piece. Roll up chicken from short end, jelly-roll style. Secure with wooden toothpicks if needed.

2. Place chicken, seam-side down, in 30 by 20 cm (12 by 8 inch) microwave-safe baking dish. Cover with vented plastic wrap; microwave on HIGH 5 min.

3. In small bowl, stir soup until smooth; stir in water, onions and thyme. Pour over chicken. Cover; microwave on HIGH 10 min or until chicken is no longer pink in centre, rotating dish once during cooking. Let stand, covered, 5 min. Makes 4 servings.

NOTE: To thaw one 284 g (10 ounce) package frozen spinach: Place frozen spinach in 1.5 L (1½ quart) microwave-safe casserole. Cover with lid; microwave on HIGH 5 min, stirring once during heating. Drain thoroughly.

■ TIP

Most of our chicken recipes suggest that you remove the chicken skin before cooking. Microwave-cooked chicken skin is usually unattractive because it doesn't brown or crisp. Removing it gives you a bonus of fewer calories too!

ROLLED CHICKEN BREASTS FLORENTINE ▶

Creamy Chicken and Vegetables

3	**whole chicken breasts, split**	**3**
25 mL	**vegetable oil**	**2 tablespoons**
1	**small onion, finely chopped**	**1**
1	**clove garlic, minced**	**1**
2 (284 mL)	**cans Campbell's Condensed Cream of Chicken Soup**	**2 (10 ounce)**
250 mL	**water**	**1 cup**
2 mL	**chili powder**	**½ teaspoon**
1 mL	**ground cumin**	**¼ teaspoon**
1 mL	**dried oregano leaves, crushed**	**¼ teaspoon**
1 mL	**black pepper**	**¼ teaspoon**
2	**medium zucchini, sliced**	**2**
1	**medium sweet red pepper, cut into strips**	**1**
1	**medium sweet green pepper, cut into strips**	**1**

1. Arrange chicken breasts in 5 L (5 quart) microwave-safe casserole, placing thicker portions toward edge of dish. In small bowl, combine oil, onion and garlic; brush onto chicken.

2. In small bowl, combine soup, water, chili powder, cumin, oregano and black pepper; pour over chicken.

3. Cover with waxed paper; microwave on HIGH 5 min.

4. Rearrange chicken breasts; add remaining ingredients. Cover; microwave on HIGH 6 min or until chicken is no longer pink in centre. Let stand, covered, 7 min. Makes 6 servings.

■ **TIP**

In high-altitude areas, food will microwave slower than in lower regions, although it may boil vigorously. Because liquids may bubble up faster, you may need a larger container for liquid mixtures such as soups. If bubbling up is still a problem, you can always remove the lid. To compensate for the lower boiling temperature and slower cooking, you may need to increase the suggested microwave power level or simply add more time to recipes. Remember that a lower boiling temperature also means liquids will evaporate quickly at high altitudes, so you may need to add more water or liquid to your recipe.

Creamed Chicken in Patty Shells

125 mL	chopped onion	½ cup
284 mL	can Campbell's Condensed Cheddar Cheese Soup	10 ounce
250 mL	grated Swiss cheese	1 cup
125 mL	milk	½ cup
50 mL	chopped pimiento	¼ cup
15 mL	dry sherry	1 tablespoon
375 mL	diced cooked chicken	1½ cups
4	Pepperidge Farm Frozen Patty Shells, baked	4

1. Place onion in 2 L (2 quart) microwave-safe casserole. Cover with lid; microwave on HIGH 1.5 min or until tender.

2. Stir in soup until smooth. Stir in cheese, milk, pimiento and sherry. Gently fold in chicken. Cover; microwave on HIGH 5 min or until hot and bubbling, stirring once during cooking. Serve over patty shells. Makes 4 servings.

Mexicali Chicken Casserole

15 mL	butter or margarine	1 tablespoon
500 mL	sliced fresh mushrooms	2 cups
125 mL	chopped onion	½ cup
284 mL	can Campbell's Condensed Nacho Cheese Soup	10 ounce
500 mL	diced cooked chicken	2 cups
2	tomatoes, chopped	2
125 mL	sour cream	½ cup
250 mL	grated Cheddar cheese	1 cup
500 mL	crushed tortilla chips	2 cups

1. In 2 L (2 quart) microwave-safe casserole, combine butter, mushrooms and onions. Cover with lid; microwave on HIGH 4 min or until vegetables are tender, stirring once during cooking.

2. Stir in soup until smooth; stir in chicken, tomatoes and sour cream. Cover; microwave on HIGH 4 min or until hot, stirring once during cooking.

3. Spread ½ of the soup mixture in 25 by 15 cm (10 by 6 inch) microwave-safe baking dish. Sprinkle with ½ of the cheese and ½ of the chips. Spread remaining soup mixture over top and sprinkle with remaining cheese.

4. Cover with waxed paper; microwave on HIGH 4 min or until cheese is melted. Let stand, covered, 2 min. Sprinkle with remaining chips. Makes 6 servings.

Turkey Meatballs

500 g	**ground turkey**	**1 pound**
1	**egg**	**1**
125 mL	**fine dry bread crumbs**	**½ cup**
50 mL	**finely chopped onion**	**¼ cup**
284 mL	**can Franco-American Chicken Gravy**	**10 ounce**
75 mL	**apple jelly**	**⅓ cup**
75 mL	**chili sauce**	**⅓ cup**
	Hot cooked thin noodles	

1. In large bowl, thoroughly mix turkey, egg, crumbs, onion and 50 mL (¼ cup) of the gravy. Shape into 2.5 cm (1 inch) meatballs; set aside.

2. In 3 L (3 quart) microwave-safe casserole, combine remaining gravy, apple jelly and chili sauce. Cover with waxed paper; microwave on HIGH 5 min or until jelly is melted, stirring once during cooking.

3. Add meatballs to gravy mixture. Cover; microwave on HIGH 8 min or until meatballs are no longer pink, stirring once during cooking. Let stand, covered, 5 min. Serve over noodles. Makes 4 servings.

Turkey Divan

500 g	**fresh or frozen broccoli spears**	**1 pound**
50 mL	**water**	**¼ cup**
284 mL	**can Campbell's Condensed Cream of Mushroom Soup**	**10 ounce**
50 mL	**milk**	**¼ cup**
15 mL	**dry sherry**	**1 tablespoon**
Dash	**ground nutmeg**	**Dash**
500 mL	**diced cooked turkey or chicken**	**2 cups**
50 mL	**grated Cheddar cheese**	**¼ cup**

1. In 25 by 15 cm (10 by 6 inch) microwave-safe casserole, combine broccoli and water. Cover with vented plastic wrap; microwave on HIGH 6 min or until broccoli is almost tender, rotating dish once during cooking. Let stand, covered, 3 min. Drain.

2. In medium bowl, stir soup until smooth. Stir in milk, sherry and nutmeg. Stir in turkey. Pour over broccoli. Sprinkle with cheese. Cover with waxed paper; microwave on HIGH 6 min or until hot, rotating dish once during cooking. Let stand, covered, 5 min. Makes 4 servings.

Turkey and Stuffing Casserole

50 mL	butter or margarine, cut up	¼ cup
1 L	herb-flavoured stuffing mix	4 cups
284 mL	can Campbell's Condensed Cream of Chicken Soup	10 ounce
125 mL	milk	½ cup
500 mL	cubed cooked turkey or chicken	2 cups
250 mL	coarsely chopped celery	1 cup
284 g	package frozen chopped broccoli, cooked and drained	10 ounce
200 mL	grated Cheddar cheese	¾ cup

1. Place butter in large microwave-safe casserole. Cover with lid; microwave on HIGH 40 sec or until melted. Add stuffing mix; toss to coat evenly. Set aside.

2. In large bowl, stir soup until smooth. Stir in milk; stir in turkey, celery and broccoli. Spread ½ of the mixture in 30 by 20 cm (12 by 8 inch) microwave-safe baking dish. Spread soup mixture over stuffing. Cover with waxed paper; microwave on HIGH 10 min or until hot, rotating dish once during cooking.

3. Top with remaining stuffing mixture; sprinkle with cheese. Microwave, uncovered, on HIGH 1 min. Let stand, uncovered, 5 min. Makes 4 servings.

Bean 'n' Chicken Tacos

15 mL	vegetable oil	1 tablespoon
125 mL	chopped onion	½ cup
15 mL	chili powder	1 tablespoon
1	clove garlic, minced	1
284 mL	can Campbell's Condensed Bean with Bacon Soup	10 ounce
125 mL	sour cream	½ cup
375 mL	diced cooked chicken	1½ cups
8	taco shells	8
	Grated Cheddar cheese	
	Shredded lettuce	
	Diced tomatoes	

1. In 2 L (2 quart) microwave-safe casserole, combine oil, onion, chili powder and garlic. Cover with lid; microwave on HIGH 2 min or until onion is tender, stirring once during cooking.

2. Stir in soup and sour cream; mix well. Cover; microwave on HIGH 3 min. Stir in chicken. Cover; microwave on HIGH 2 min or until hot and bubbling.

3. Spoon about 50 mL (¼ cup) of the chicken mixture into each taco shell. Top with remaining ingredients. Makes 8 tacos or 4 servings.

Glazed Stuffed Cornish Hens

2 (750 g)	**Cornish hens**	**2 (1½ pounds)**
50 mL	**butter or margarine**	**¼ cup**
125 mL	**chopped onion**	**½ cup**
125 mL	**sweet red pepper, cut into julienne strips**	**½ cup**
125 mL	**green pepper, cut into julienne strips**	**½ cup**
1 L	**herb-flavoured stuffing mix**	**4 cups**
125 mL	**Campbell's Condensed Chicken Broth**	**½ cup**
125 mL	**water**	**½ cup**
125 mL	**apricot jam**	**½ cup**

1. Remove giblets and neck from inside hens (reserve for another use if desired). Rinse hens; pat dry. Split hens along backbone and breastbone; set aside.

2. In 3 L (3 quart) microwave-safe casserole, combine butter, onion and peppers. Cover with vented plastic wrap; microwave on HIGH 3 min or until vegetables are tender, stirring once during cooking. Add stuffing, broth and water; toss to mix well.

3. Pat stuffing mixture onto bottom of 30 by 20 cm (12 by 8 inch) microwave-safe baking dish. Arrange hen halves, skin-side up, over stuffing; set aside.

4. Place jam in small microwave-safe bowl. Microwave, uncovered, on HIGH 45 sec or until melted. Brush jam over hens. Cover with waxed paper; microwave on HIGH 17 min or until hens are no longer pink in centre, rotating dish twice and rearranging hens once during cooking. Let stand, covered, 5 min. Makes 4 servings.

■ **TIP**

Freeze small amounts of leftover chicken broth, pesto or tomato sauce in ice cube trays. When frozen, store cubes in a freezer bag until ready to use. To use, microwave 1 or 2 cubes in a custard cup until melted.

GLAZED STUFFED CORNISH HENS▶

Chicken Potato Topper

250 mL	**chopped carrots**	**1 cup**
125 mL	**thinly sliced celery**	**½ cup**
50 mL	**chopped onion**	**¼ cup**
15 mL	**water**	**1 tablespoon**
284 mL	**can Campbell's Condensed Cream of Mushroom Soup**	**10 ounce**
75 mL	**milk**	**⅓ cup**
Dash	**pepper**	**Dash**
Dash	**rubbed sage**	**Dash**
250 mL	**diced cooked chicken**	**1 cup**
3	**hot baked potatoes, split**	**3**
125 mL	**grated Cheddar cheese**	**½ cup**

1. In 1.5 L (1½ quart) microwave-safe casserole, combine carrots, celery, onion and water. Cover with lid; microwave on HIGH 5 min or until vegetables are tender, stirring once during cooking.

2. Stir in soup, milk, pepper and sage. Cover; microwave on HIGH 3 min or until hot. Gently stir in chicken. Cover; microwave on HIGH 2 min or until hot and bubbling. Spoon chicken mixture over potatoes. Top with cheese. Makes 3 servings.

NOTE: To cook potatoes: Pierce 3 baking potatoes (250 g [8 ounces] each) with fork in several places. Arrange in circular pattern on microwave-safe plate. Microwave, uncovered, on HIGH 8 min or until tender, rearranging potatoes once during cooking. Let stand while preparing topper.

■ **TIP**

When you're barbecuing foods (such as chicken, ribs, burgers or hot dogs) outdoors, make each session count double. Cook twice as much food as you expect to eat, then freeze or refrigerate the rest. Later, heat in the microwave oven for food that tastes as if it just came off the grill.

Chicken and Ham Supreme

284 g	**package frozen asparagus cuts**	**10 ounce**
284 mL	**can Campbell's Condensed Cream of Mushroom Soup**	**10 ounce**
125 mL	**plain yogurt**	**½ cup**
125 mL	**grated Swiss cheese**	**½ cup**
5 mL	**dried basil leaves, crushed**	**1 teaspoon**
Dash	**cayenne pepper**	**Dash**
500 mL	**cooked rice**	**2 cups**
375 mL	**diced cooked chicken**	**1½ cups**
250 mL	**diced cooked ham**	**1 cup**
	Chopped fresh parsley for garnish	

1. Place asparagus in 1 L (1 quart) microwave-safe casserole. Cover with lid; microwave on HIGH 4 min or until hot, stirring once during cooking. Drain; set aside.

2. In small bowl, stir soup until smooth; stir in yogurt, cheese, basil and cayenne.

3. In 20 by 20 cm (8 by 8 inch) microwave-safe baking dish, combine rice and 125 mL (½ cup) of the soup mixture; spread evenly in dish. Top with chicken, ham and asparagus. Spoon remaining soup mixture over top.

4. Cover with vented plastic wrap; microwave on HIGH 8 min or until hot, rotating dish once during cooking. Let stand, covered, 2 min. Garnish with parsley. Makes 4 servings.

■ TIP

Even if you never buy a utensil designed for the microwave oven, your shelves are probably full of them: glass measuring cups; glass and ceramic casseroles and mixing bowls; mugs, teacups, bowls and plates made of microwave-safe china; glass and ceramic pie plates and baking dishes.

Creamy Chicken Enchiladas

375 mL	**diced cooked chicken**	**1½ cups**
125 mL	**chopped tomato**	**½ cup**
25 mL	**chopped green chilies**	**2 tablespoons**
2 mL	**dried oregano leaves, crushed**	**½ teaspoon**
284 mL	**can Campbell's Condensed Cream of Chicken or Cream of Mushroom Soup**	**10 ounce**
125 mL	**sour cream**	**½ cup**
75 mL	**enchilada sauce**	**⅓ cup**
15 mL	**lemon juice**	**1 tablespoon**
8 (15 cm)	**corn tortillas**	**8 (6 inch)**
250 mL	**grated Cheddar cheese**	**1 cup**
	Chopped tomatoes for garnish	
	Chopped lettuce for garnish	
	Sliced pitted ripe olives for garnish	

1. In small bowl, combine chicken, tomato, chilies and oregano; set aside.

2. In 1 L (1 quart) microwave-safe casserole, stir soup until smooth. Stir in sour cream, enchilada sauce and lemon juice. Cover with lid; microwave at 50% power 5 min or until hot, stirring once during cooking. Stir 250 mL (1 cup) of the soup mixture into the chicken mixture; set aside.

3. Wrap stack of tortillas in damp paper towels; microwave on HIGH 1 min or until warm. Spoon 50 mL (¼ cup) of chicken mixture along centre of each tortilla; roll up.

4. Arrange filled tortillas in 30 by 20 cm (12 by 8 inch) microwave-safe baking dish. Pour remaining soup mixture over tortillas. Cover with vented plastic wrap; microwave on HIGH 8 min or until hot, rotating dish once during cooking.

5. Sprinkle with cheese. Microwave, uncovered, on HIGH 1 min or until cheese is melted. Garnish with tomatoes, lettuce and olives. Makes 4 servings.

■ **TIP**

For a special touch after a meal, make warm finger towels. Fold clean wet washcloths in half, then roll up and place in a microwave-safe basket. Microwave on HIGH about 30 sec. These are also great for cleaning your hands after eating ribs or chicken.

Chicken Spaghetti Marinara

15 mL	**vegetable oil**	**1 tablespoon**
250 mL	**sliced fresh mushrooms**	**1 cup**
250 mL	**sliced zucchini**	**1 cup**
50 mL	**chopped onion**	**¼ cup**
1	**clove garlic, minced**	**1**
450 mL	**Prego Spaghetti Sauce**	**1¾ cups**
250 mL	**cubed cooked chicken**	**1 cup**
5 mL	**lemon juice**	**1 teaspoon**
	Hot cooked spaghetti	

1. In a 2 L (2 quart) microwave-safe casserole, combine oil, mushrooms, zucchini, onion and garlic. Cover with lid; microwave on HIGH 5 min or until vegetables are tender-crisp, stirring once during cooking.

2. Stir in spaghetti sauce, chicken and lemon juice. Microwave on HIGH 5 min or until heated through, stirring once during cooking.

3. Serve over spaghetti. Makes 4 servings.

Chicken Tetrazzini

Here's a quick way to dress up leftover chicken or turkey for a speedy meal anytime!

284 mL	**can Franco-American Chicken Gravy**	**10 ounce**
125 mL	**light cream**	**½ cup**
25 mL	**dry sherry**	**2 tablespoons**
15 mL	**lemon juice**	**1 tablespoon**
500 mL	**sliced fresh mushrooms**	**2 cups**
175 g	**spaghetti, cooked and drained**	**6 ounces**
50 mL	**chopped pimiento**	**¼ cup**
125 mL	**grated Parmesan cheese**	**½ cup**
375 mL	**diced cooked chicken or turkey**	**1½ cups**

1. In 3 L (3 quart) microwave-safe casserole, combine gravy, cream, sherry and lemon juice. Cover with lid; microwave on HIGH 2 min or until hot.

2. Stir in mushrooms, spaghetti, pimiento and 50 mL (¼ cup) of the Parmesan cheese. Stir in chicken. Cover; microwave on HIGH 7 min or until hot, stirring once during cooking.

3. Top with remaining 50 mL (¼ cup) cheese. Microwave, uncovered, on HIGH 2 min. Let stand, uncovered, 2 min. Makes 4 servings.

Fish and Seafood

Salmon Steaks in Dill Sauce

15 mL	butter or margarine	1 tablespoon
125 mL	chopped green onions	½ cup
284 mL	can Campbell's Condensed Cream of Celery Soup	10 ounce
125 mL	half-and-half	½ cup
50 mL	Chablis or other dry white wine	¼ cup
25 mL	chopped fresh dill weed	2 tablespoons
	OR	
5 mL	dried dill weed, crushed	1 teaspoon
4	salmon steaks (about 2 cm [¾ inch] thick)	4

1. In 30 by 20 cm (12 by 8 inch) microwave-safe baking dish, combine butter and onions. Cover with vented plastic wrap; microwave on HIGH 2 min or until onions are tender, stirring once during cooking.

2. Stir in soup until smooth. Stir in half-and-half, Chablis and dill; blend well.

3. Arrange salmon steaks in sauce, placing thicker portions toward edges of dish. Cover; microwave on HIGH 9 min or until fish flakes easily when tested with fork, rotating dish twice during cooking. Let stand, covered, 5 min. Garnish with additional dill weed if desired. Makes 4 servings.

SALMON STEAKS IN DILL SAUCE ▶

A dry
ALMADEN
Vineyards

Mediterranean Cod

284 mL	can Campbell's Condensed Cream of Potato Soup	10 ounce
50 mL	milk	¼ cup
2	green onions, thinly sliced	2
25 mL	lemon juice	2 tablespoons
10 mL	dry mustard	2 teaspoons
1	clove garlic, minced	1
284 g	package frozen fish fillets	10 ounce
	Chopped fresh parsley for garnish	
	Freshly ground pepper for garnish	

1. In 20 by 20 cm (8 by 8 inch) microwave-safe baking dish, stir soup until smooth. Stir in milk, onions, lemon juice, mustard and garlic. Cover with vented plastic wrap; microwave on HIGH 3 min or until hot and bubbling, stirring once during cooking.

2. Arrange frozen fillets over sauce. Cover; microwave on HIGH 8 min or until fish flakes easily when tested with fork, rearranging fish and spooning sauce over once during cooking. Let stand, covered, 3 min. Garnish with parsley and pepper. Makes 2 servings.

NOTE: You may use cod, sole, Boston bluefish or turbot.

Fish with Mushroom Sauce

284 mL	can Campbell's Condensed Cream of Mushroom Soup	10 ounce
50 mL	sour cream	¼ cup
10 mL	dry sherry	2 teaspoons
2 mL	dried dill weed, crushed	½ teaspoon
Dash	pepper	Dash
500 mL	cooked rice	2 cups
284 g	package frozen chopped broccoli, thawed and drained	10 ounce
4	halibut or salmon steaks (about 750 g [1½ pounds])	4
4	thin slices red onion	4

1. In 1 L (4 cup) glass measure, combine soup, sour cream, sherry, dill and pepper. In medium bowl, combine rice, broccoli and 125 mL (½ cup) of the soup mixture.

2. In 22.5 by 22.5 cm (9 by 9 inch) microwave-safe baking dish, arrange rice mixture. Arrange fish over top, placing thicker portions toward edges of dish. Top with onions. Cover with waxed paper; microwave on HIGH 10 min or until fish flakes easily when tested with fork, rotating dish twice during cooking. Let stand, covered, while cooking sauce.

3. Meanwhile, microwave remaining soup mixture on HIGH 4 min or until hot. Serve with fish. Makes 4 servings.

Crab-Stuffed Sole Fillets

284 g	**package individually quick-frozen fish fillets**	**10 ounce**
25 mL	**butter or margarine**	**2 tablespoons**
25 mL	**chopped green onion**	**2 tablespoons**
125 mL	**chopped fresh mushrooms**	**½ cup**
50 mL	**chopped celery**	**¼ cup**
200 g	**can crabmeat, drained and cartilage removed**	**7.1 ounce**
284 mL	**can Campbell's Condensed Cream of Celery or Cream of Chicken Soup**	**10 ounce**
75 mL	**milk**	**⅓ cup**
25 mL	**Chablis or other dry white wine**	**2 tablespoons**
125 mL	**grated Swiss cheese**	**½ cup**

1. Separate fish fillets. Arrange on microwave-safe plate. Microwave, uncovered, on HIGH 1 min or until fish is pliable. Set aside.

2. To make stuffing: In 1 L (1 quart) microwave-safe casserole, combine butter, onion, mushrooms and celery. Cover with vented plastic wrap; microwave on HIGH 2 min or until vegetables are tender. Stir in crabmeat and 25 mL (2 tablespoons) of the soup. Make 4 mounds of stuffing in 25 cm (10 inch) microwave-safe pie plate. Divide fillets into 4 parts and arrange over stuffing; set aside.

3. In 500 mL (2 cup) glass measure, stir remaining soup mixture until smooth. Stir in milk, Chablis and cheese. Microwave, uncovered, on HIGH 3 min or until cheese is melted, stirring once during cooking.

4. Pour soup mixture over fish. Cover with waxed paper; microwave on HIGH 6 min or until fish flakes easily when tested with fork, rotating dish once during cooking. Let stand, covered, 5 min. Makes 4 servings.

NOTE: You may use sole, cod or whitefish.

■ TIP

If you are going to use your microwave oven to cook more than one dish for a meal, follow these guidelines:

- Cook only one dish at a time. If two are cooked together, they will interfere with the microwave absorption of each other.
- The first dish cooked should be the one with the longer cooking time and the one that can retain its heat longer. Generally, denser foods, such as casseroles, stews and meats, hold heat better.
- If one food cools before serving, reheat it briefly.
- If a dessert can be served warm, cook it during the meal.

Flounder Roll-Ups

15 mL	butter or margarine	1 tablespoon
50 mL	chopped onion	¼ cup
1	clove garlic, minced	1
450 mL	Prego Spaghetti Sauce	1¾ cups
75 mL	grated carrot	⅓ cup
75 mL	grated zucchini	⅓ cup
75 mL	ricotta cheese	⅓ cup
15 mL	toasted, chopped pine nuts (optional)	1 tablespoon
4	sole or flounder fillets (about 500 g [1 pound])	4
	Lemon wedges	
	Grated Parmesan cheese	
	Hot cooked spinach linguine	

1. In 25 by 15 cm (10 by 6 inch) microwave-safe baking dish, combine butter, onion and garlic. Cover with vented plastic wrap; microwave on HIGH 2 min or until onion is tender-crisp. Stir in spaghetti sauce.

2. To prepare fish roll-ups: In small bowl, combine carrot, zucchini, ricotta cheese and pine nuts. Spoon about 25 mL (2 tablespoons) of the mixture onto centre of each fillet; roll up. Secure with wooden toothpicks if necessary.

3. Arrange roll-ups, seam-side down, in sauce. Spoon about 15 mL (1 tablespoon) sauce over each roll-up. Cover; microwave on HIGH 6 min or until fish flakes easily when tested with fork.

4. Serve with lemon wedges, Parmesan and linguine. Makes 4 servings.

Basil-Pepper Flounder

1	medium green pepper, cut into strips	1
125 mL	sliced onion	½ cup
500 g	flounder or sole fillets	1 pound
200 mL	V8 Vegetable Juice	¾ cup
2 mL	dried basil leaves, crushed	½ teaspoon
500 mL	hot cooked rice	2 cups

1. In 30 by 20 cm (12 by 8 inch) microwave-safe baking dish, combine pepper and onion. Cover with vented plastic wrap; microwave on HIGH 5 min or until just tender, rotating dish once. Drain.

2. Arrange fish fillets in single layer over vegetables. Combine V8 juice and basil; pour over fish.

3. Cover; microwave on HIGH 5 min or until fish flakes easily when tested with fork, rotating dish once during cooking. Serve with rice. Makes 4 servings.

FLOUNDER ROLL-UPS ▶

Snapper with Garden Vegetables

1	whole red snapper (about 1 kg [2 pounds]), dressed, with head and tail on	1
15 mL	lime juice	1 tablespoon
15 mL	butter or margarine	1 tablespoon
125 mL	celery, cut into julienne strips	½ cup
125 mL	carrot, cut into julienne strips	½ cup
125 mL	zucchini, cut into julienne strips	½ cup
284 mL	can Campbell's Condensed Cream of Celery Soup	10 ounce
125 mL	milk	½ cup
1	clove garlic, minced	1
25 mL	pimiento, cut into julienne strips	2 tablespoons

1. Rinse fish; pat dry with paper towel. Pierce eyes with toothpick. Brush fish inside and out with lime juice; set aside.

2. In 1 L (1 quart) microwave-safe casserole, combine butter, celery and carrot. Cover with lid; microwave on HIGH 2 min. Stir in zucchini. Cover; microwave on HIGH 1 min or until vegetables are tender-crisp. Stir 50 mL (¼ cup) of the soup into vegetables.

3. Place fish on large microwave-safe platter. Spoon vegetables into cavity of fish. Cover with vented plastic wrap; microwave at 50% power 20 min or until fish flakes easily when tested with fork, rotating dish twice during cooking. Let stand, covered while preparing sauce.

4. To make sauce: In 500 mL (2 cup) glass measure, stir remaining soup until smooth; stir in milk, garlic and pimiento. Cover with vented plastic wrap; microwave on HIGH 3 min or until hot and bubbling, stirring once during cooking. Spoon some sauce over fish, pass remaining sauce. Makes 3 servings.

NOTE: Substitute two 500 g (1 pound) fish for snapper. Divide vegetables between the fish. Place both fish on large microwave-safe platter. Microwave as directed.

NOTE: Fish eyes will become cloudy. If desired, cover with halved grape or olive slice after cooking.

■ **TIP**

Never put into the microwave oven the twist ties that come with plastic storage bags and some types of bread. The combination of wire and paper could cause arcing and could ignite. For the same reason, don't put tea bags with metal staples in your microwave oven.

SNAPPER WITH GARDEN VEGETABLES▶

Salmon and Spinach Pie

For maximum calcium value, don't remove the bones from the salmon; just mash them with the fish. The soft bones will blend well with the rest of the dish.

425 g	**can salmon, drained and flaked**	**15 ounce**
75 mL	**fine dry bread crumbs**	**⅓ cup**
15 mL	**lemon juice**	**1 tablespoon**
Dash	**pepper**	**Dash**
284 mL	**can Campbell's Condensed Cream of Celery Soup**	**10 ounce**
3	**eggs**	**3**
284 g	**package frozen chopped spinach, thawed and well drained (see Note on page 34)**	**10 ounce**
1 mL	**ground nutmeg**	**¼ teaspoon**

1. In medium bowl, thoroughly mix salmon, crumbs, lemon juice, pepper, ⅓ of the soup and 1 of the eggs. Spread evenly in 22.5 cm (9 inch) microwave-safe pie plate. Cover with waxed paper; microwave on HIGH 3 min or until hot, rotating dish once during cooking.

2. Meanwhile, in same bowl, stir remaining soup until smooth; stir in remaining 2 eggs, spinach and nutmeg. Spread evenly over salmon mixture.

3. Elevate dish, if necessary (see page 7). Microwave, uncovered, at 50% power 20 min or until centre is set, rotating dish twice during cooking. Let stand, uncovered, 5 min. Makes 6 servings.

■ TIP

Cut down on preparation time later. Bake an entire package of brown-and-serve rolls in your conventional oven, even if you won't use them all at once. Wrap and freeze leftovers. Later, warm just what you need in the microwave oven.

Tuna-Pasta Casserole

250 mL	**frozen peas**	**1 cup**
284 mL	**can Campbell's Condensed Cream of Celery Soup**	**10 ounce**
125 mL	**milk**	**½ cup**
125 mL	**grated Swiss cheese**	**½ cup**
198 g	**can tuna, drained and flaked**	**7 ounce**
500 mL	**cooked corkscrew or other macaroni**	**2 cups**
2	**hard-cooked eggs, chopped**	**2**
125 mL	**crushed potato chips**	**½ cup**

1. Place peas in 1 L (1 quart) microwave-safe casserole. Cover with lid; microwave on HIGH 4 min or until tender. Drain; set aside.

2. In 1.5 L (1½ quart) microwave-safe casserole, stir soup until smooth. Stir in milk and cheese. Fold in tuna, macaroni, eggs and peas. Cover; microwave on HIGH 7 min or until hot and bubbling, stirring once during cooking. Let stand, covered, 5 min.

3. Sprinkle potato chips over casserole. Makes 4 servings.

Pasta with Clam Sauce

284 mL	**can Campbell's Condensed Cream of Mushroom or Cream of Celery Soup**	**10 ounce**
170 g	**can minced clams, undrained**	**6 ounce**
50 mL	**milk**	**¼ cup**
50 mL	**Chablis or other dry white wine**	**¼ cup**
25 mL	**chopped fresh parsley**	**2 tablespoons**
25 mL	**grated Parmesan cheese**	**2 tablespoons**
1	**large clove garlic, minced**	**1**
250 g	**linguine, cooked and drained**	**8 ounces**

1. In 1.5 L (1½ quart) microwave-safe casserole, stir soup until smooth. Stir in clams, milk, Chablis, parsley, Parmesan and garlic. Cover with lid; microwave on HIGH 8 min or until hot and bubbling, stirring once during cooking.

2. Toss with linguine. Serve with additional Parmesan. Makes 4 servings.

Fish Stew

284 g	package frozen cod fillets	10 ounce
12	mussels	12
	OR	
250 g	bay scallops or halved sea scallops	½ pound
250 mL	sliced celery	1 cup
284 mL	can Campbell's Condensed Chicken Broth	10 ounce
½	soup can water	½
450 mL	Prego Spaghetti Sauce	1¾ cups
250 g	medium shrimp, shelled and deveined	½ pound

1. Separate fish fillets. Arrange fish on microwave-safe plate. Microwave, uncovered, on HIGH 1 min or until fish is pliable. Cut fish into 2.5 cm (1 inch) pieces. Set aside. Discard any mussels that do not start to close when lightly tapped. Scrub mussels under cold running water; remove and discard beards.

2. In 3 L (3 quart) microwave-safe casserole, combine celery and 50 mL (¼ cup) of the broth. Cover with lid; microwave on HIGH 3 min or until celery is tender, stirring once during cooking. Stir in remaining broth, water and spaghetti sauce. Cover; microwave on HIGH 5 min or until very hot.

3. Add fish, mussels and shrimp to hot mixture. Cover; microwave on HIGH 8 min or until fish flakes easily with fork and mussels open. Discard any unopened mussels. Makes 4 servings.

Shrimp Fettucini

125 mL	carrot, cut into julienne strips	½ cup
125 mL	celery, cut into julienne strips	½ cup
2	cloves garlic, minced	2
2 mL	dried dill weed, crushed	½ teaspoon
284 mL	can Campbell's Condensed Cream of Celery Soup	10 ounce
125 mL	milk	½ cup
250 g	medium shrimp, shelled and deveined	½ pound
175 g	fettucini, cooked and drained	6 ounces
75 mL	grated Parmesan cheese	⅓ cup
15 mL	lemon juice	1 tablespoon

1. In 3 L (3 quart) microwave-safe casserole, combine carrot, celery, garlic and dill. Cover with lid; microwave on HIGH 3 min or until vegetables are tender-crisp, stirring once during cooking.

2. Stir in soup until smooth. Stir in remaining ingredients. Cover; microwave at 50% power 15 min or until shrimp are pink, stirring twice during cooking. Let stand, covered, 5 min. Makes 4 servings.

FISH STEW ▶

Simple Shrimp Creole

15 mL	**butter or margarine**	**1 tablespoon**
125 mL	**chopped onion**	**½ cup**
1	**medium green pepper, cut into julienne strips**	**1**
125 mL	**thinly sliced celery**	**½ cup**
450 mL	**Prego Spaghetti Sauce**	**1¾ cups**
375 g	**medium shrimp, shelled and deveined**	**¾ pound**
1	**bay leaf**	**1**
Dash	**black pepper**	**Dash**
Dash	**hot pepper sauce**	**Dash**
	Hot cooked rice	

1. In 2 L (2 quart) microwave-safe casserole, combine butter, onion, green pepper and celery. Cover with lid; microwave on HIGH 4 min or until vegetables are tender, stirring once during cooking.

2. Stir in spaghetti sauce, shrimp, bay leaf, black pepper and hot pepper sauce. Cover; microwave on HIGH 6 min or until shrimp are pink, stirring once during cooking. Let stand, covered, 5 min. Remove bay leaf. Serve over rice. Makes 4 servings.

Cajun Shrimp

4	**slices bacon, diced**	**4**
25 mL	**all-purpose flour**	**2 tablespoons**
1	**medium onion, chopped**	**1**
125 mL	**chopped celery**	**½ cup**
125 mL	**chopped green pepper**	**½ cup**
1	**large clove garlic, minced**	**1**
2 mL	**dried thyme leaves, crushed**	**½ teaspoon**
375 mL	**V8 Vegetable Juice**	**1½ cups**
15 mL	**Louisiana-style hot sauce**	**1 tablespoon**
500 g	**large shrimp, shelled and deveined**	**1 pound**
	Hot cooked rice	

1. Place bacon in 2 L (2 quart) microwave-safe casserole. Cover with paper towel. Microwave on HIGH 4 min or until crisp. Transfer bacon to paper towels to drain, reserving 25 mL (2 tablespoons) of the drippings in casserole.

2. Stir flour into drippings. Cover with lid; microwave on HIGH 1 min.

3. Stir in onion, celery, pepper, garlic and thyme. Cover; microwave on HIGH 4 min or until vegetables are tender, stirring once during cooking.

4. Stir in V8 juice, hot pepper sauce and shrimp. Cover; microwave on HIGH 6 min or until shrimp are pink, stirring once during cooking. Let stand, covered, 5 min. Serve over rice. Garnish with reserved bacon. Makes 4 servings.

Jambalaya

25 mL	olive oil or bacon drippings	2 tablespoons
250 mL	chopped onion	1 cup
250 mL	chopped green pepper	1 cup
1	large clove garlic, minced	1
250 g	skinless, boneless raw chicken, cut into 2.5 cm (1 inch) pieces	½ pound
125 g	smoked sausage, cut into 1.5 cm (½ inch) pieces	¼ pound
125 mL	regular long-grain rice, uncooked	½ cup
375 mL	V8 Vegetable Juice	1½ cups
5 mL	hot pepper sauce	1 teaspoon
1 mL	dried thyme leaves, crushed	¼ teaspoon
1	bay leaf	1
250 g	medium shrimp, shelled and deveined	½ pound
50 mL	chopped fresh parsley	¼ cup

1. In 3 L (3 quart) microwave-safe casserole, combine oil, onion, green pepper and garlic. Cover with lid; microwave on HIGH 4 min or until vegetables are tender, stirring once during cooking.

2. Stir in chicken, sausage, rice, V8 juice, hot pepper sauce, thyme and bay leaf. Cover; microwave on HIGH 10 min or until bubbling, stirring once during cooking. Stir again.

3. Reduce power to 50%. Cover; microwave 10 min or until rice is nearly done. Stir in shrimp and parsley. Cover; microwave at 50% power 5 min or until shrimp are pink, stirring once during cooking. Let stand, covered, 5 min. Remove bay leaf. Makes 6 servings.

■ **TIP**

When a food container is described as "microwave only" never put it in a conventional oven, not even to keep the food warm at a very low setting. These containers can melt or scorch at very low temperatures. (The same applies to microwave-only cookware.)

Mediterranean Seafood Sauce

50 mL	**thinly sliced celery**	**1/4 cup**
15 mL	**butter or margarine**	**1 tablespoon**
1	**clove garlic, minced**	**1**
450 mL	**Prego Spaghetti Sauce**	**1 3/4 cups**
50 mL	**Chablis or other dry white wine**	**1/4 cup**
250 g	**bay scallops**	**1/2 pound**
250 g	**medium shrimp, shelled and deveined (15 to 20 per 500 g [1 pound])**	**1/2 pound**
	Hot cooked fettucini	
	Chopped fresh parsley	

1. In 2 L (2 quart) microwave-safe casserole, combine celery, butter and garlic. Cover with lid; microwave on HIGH 3 min or until celery is tender.

2. Stir in spaghetti sauce and Chablis. Cover; microwave on HIGH 4 min or until sauce is hot.

3. Stir in scallops and shrimp. Cover; microwave on HIGH 4 min or until scallops are opaque and shrimp are pink. Let stand, covered, 2 min.

4. Stir before serving. Serve over fettucini. Garnish with parsley. Makes 4 servings.

Scallops in Cream Sauce

15 mL	**butter or margarine**	**1 tablespoon**
250 mL	**sliced fresh mushrooms**	**1 cup**
25 mL	**sliced green onion**	**2 tablespoons**
1	**clove garlic, minced**	**1**
284 mL	**can Campbell's Condensed Cream of Celery Soup**	**10 ounce**
500 g	**bay scallops or halved sea scallops**	**1 pound**
25 mL	**Chablis or other dry white wine**	**2 tablespoons**
20 mL	**grated Parmesan cheese**	**4 teaspoons**
	Paprika for garnish	

1. In 1.5 L (1 1/2 quart) microwave-safe casserole, combine butter, mushrooms, onion and garlic. Cover with lid; microwave on HIGH 3 min or until vegetables are tender, stirring once during cooking.

2. Stir in soup until smooth. Stir in scallops and wine. Microwave, uncovered, on HIGH 10 min or until scallops are opaque, stirring twice during cooking. Let stand, uncovered, 2 min. Divide among 4 individual serving dishes or shells. Sprinkle with cheese and paprika. Makes 4 servings.

MEDITERRANEAN SEAFOOD SAUCE▶

Beef, Pork and Lamb

Shepherd's Pie

For a festive touch, use a pastry tube to pipe the mashed potatoes around the edge of the dish.

15 mL	**butter or margarine**	**1 tablespoon**
250 mL	**thinly sliced carrots**	**1 cup**
125 mL	**chopped onion**	**½ cup**
284 mL	**can Franco-American Beef Gravy**	**10 ounce**
375 mL	**cubed cooked beef**	**1½ cups**
500 mL	**hot mashed potatoes**	**2 cups**
	OR	
	Microwave Mashed Potatoes (recipe follows)	
50 mL	**grated Cheddar cheese**	**¼ cup**

1. In 2 L (2 quart) microwave-safe casserole, combine butter, carrots and onion. Cover with lid; microwave on HIGH 5 min or until vegetables are almost tender, stirring once during cooking.

2. Stir in gravy and beef. Cover; microwave on HIGH 5 min or until bubbling, stirring once during cooking.

3. Spoon potatoes around edge of casserole; sprinkle with cheese. Microwave, uncovered, on HIGH 3 min or until cheese is melted. Makes 4 servings.

Microwave Mashed Potatoes: With fork, pierce 3 medium potatoes (500 g [1 pound]) in circular pattern on microwave-safe plate. Microwave, uncovered, on HIGH 7 min or until tender, rearranging potatoes once during cooking. Scoop potato pulp from skins, discarding skins. In medium bowl, combine potato pulp, 50 mL (¼ cup) milk, 15 mL (1 tablespoon) butter or margarine and 1 mL (¼ teaspoon) salt. With electric mixer or potato masher, mash until smooth.

SHEPHERD'S PIE ▶

Souper Pot Roast

25 mL	all-purpose flour	2 tablespoons
1.5 kg	beef chuck roast	3 pound
284 mL	can Campbell's Condensed Cream of Mushroom Soup	10 ounce
1	bay leaf	1
4	carrots, peeled and cut into 5 cm (2 inch) lengths	4
2	large potatoes, quartered	2

1. Place flour in 3 L (3 quart) microwave-safe casserole. Add roast; turn to coat with flour on all sides. Discard excess flour. Spread soup over meat; add bay leaf. Cover with lid; microwave on HIGH 20 min.

2. Turn roast, spooning soup over meat. Reduce power to 50%. Cover; microwave 20 min.

3. Add carrots and potatoes to casserole. Cover; microwave at 50% power 40 min or until meat and vegetables are tender, rotating dish once during cooking. Let stand, covered, 10 min. Remove bay leaf. Makes 6 servings.

Beef Ragoût

15 mL	butter or margarine	1 tablespoon
125 mL	chopped onion	½ cup
1	large clove garlic, minced	1
500 g	stew beef, cut into 2.5 cm (1 inch) cubes	1 pound
250 mL	thinly sliced carrots	1 cup
284 mL	can Franco-American Beef Gravy	10 ounce
50 mL	Burgundy or other dry red wine	¼ cup
50 mL	tomato paste	¼ cup
	Hot cooked noodles	

1. In 2 L (2 quart) microwave-safe casserole, combine butter, onion and garlic. Cover with lid; microwave on HIGH 3 min or until onion is tender, stirring once during cooking.

2. Stir in beef. Cover; microwave on HIGH 5 min or until beef is no longer pink, stirring once during cooking.

3. Stir in carrots, gravy, Burgundy and tomato paste. Cover; microwave on HIGH 5 min or until boiling. Stir again.

4. Reduce power to 50%. Cover; microwave 30 min or until meat is tender, stirring twice during cooking. Let stand, covered, 5 min. Serve over noodles. Makes 4 servings.

NOTE: It's often more economical to buy a chuck steak or roast than to buy "beef for stew." You have the advantage of controlling the size of the pieces when you trim and cut meat yourself.

Vegetable-Stuffed Flank Steak

15 mL	**olive or vegetable oil**	**1 tablespoon**
250 mL	**chopped fresh mushrooms**	**1 cup**
284 g	**package frozen chopped spinach, thawed and well drained (see Note on page 34)**	**10 ounce**
125 mL	**chopped onion**	**½ cup**
1	**clove garlic, minced**	**1**
250 mL	**grated carrots**	**1 cup**
125 mL	**grated Swiss cheese**	**½ cup**
2 mL	**dried basil leaves, crushed**	**½ teaspoon**
Dash	**pepper**	**Dash**
750 g	**beef flank steak, pounded to 1 cm (¼ inch) thickness**	**1½ pounds**
284 mL	**can Campbell's Condensed Cream of Mushroom Soup**	**10 ounce**
25 mL	**dry sherry**	**2 tablespoons**

1. In 1.5 L (1½ quart) microwave-safe casserole, combine oil, mushrooms, spinach, onion and garlic. Cover with lid; microwave on HIGH 5 min or until vegetables are tender, stirring once during cooking. Drain. Stir in carrots, cheese, basil and pepper.

2. Spread vegetable mixture over steak to within 2.5 cm (1 inch) of edges. Roll up from long end, jelly-roll fashion, tucking ends of steak into roll. Secure with wooden toothpicks or tie with cotton string. Place roll, seam-side down, in 30 by 20 cm (12 by 8 inch) microwave-safe baking dish.

3. In small bowl, stir soup until smooth; stir in sherry. Pour over meat. Cover with vented plastic wrap; microwave on HIGH 10 min, rotating dish once during cooking.

4. Spoon pan juices over meat. Reduce power to 50%. Cover; microwave 20 min or until meat is tender, rotating dish twice during cooking. Let stand, covered, 10 min. Makes 6 servings.

■ **TIP**

To reheat leftover roast beef, turkey or other cooked meat in gravy: In 2 L (2 quart) microwave-safe casserole, pour one 284 mL (10 ounce) can Franco-American Beef, Chicken or Mushroom Gravy over 500g (1 pound) sliced cooked meat. Cover with lid; microwave on HIGH 3 min or until hot, rotating dish once during cooking. This is also a great way to make hot roast beef or turkey sandwiches.

Ginger Beef

375 g	**beef flank steak**	**¾ pound**
284 mL	**can Campbell's Condensed Tomato Soup**	**10 ounce**
75 mL	**water**	**⅓ cup**
25 mL	**peanut or vegetable oil**	**2 tablespoons**
15 mL	**soy sauce**	**1 tablespoon**
2 mL	**ground ginger**	**½ teaspoon**
1	**clove garlic, minced**	**1**
1	**medium green pepper, cut into 2.5 cm (1 inch) squares**	**1**
250 mL	**broccoli flowerets**	**1 cup**
	Hot cooked rice	

1. Freeze steak 1 h to make slicing easier. Cut steak across the grain into very thin slices.

2. In 30 by 20 cm (12 by 8 inch) microwave-safe baking dish, combine soup, water, oil, soy sauce, ginger and garlic. Add beef slices; toss to coat well. Cover; refrigerate at least 1 h.

3. Cover with vented plastic wrap; microwave on HIGH 6 min or until beef is no longer pink, stirring twice during cooking.

4. Add pepper and broccoli. Cover; microwave on HIGH 5 min or until vegetables are tender, stirring twice during cooking. Serve over rice. Makes 4 servings.

Beef Stroganoff

500 g	**boneless sirloin steak**	**1 pound**
125 mL	**chopped onion**	**½ cup**
284 mL	**can Campbell's Condensed Cream of Mushroom Soup**	**10 ounce**
125 mL	**sour cream**	**½ cup**
2 mL	**paprika**	**½ teaspoon**
	Hot cooked noodles	

1. Freeze steak 1 hour to make slicing easier. Cut steak across the grain into very thin slices.

2. In 2 L (2 quart) microwave-safe casserole, combine beef and onion. Cover with lid; microwave on HIGH 5 min or until beef is no longer pink, stirring once during cooking.

3. In small bowl, stir soup until smooth; stir in sour cream and paprika. Add to beef, stirring to coat. Cover; microwave at 50% power 3 min or until hot. Serve over noodles. Makes about 4 servings.

Beef Stir-Fry in Creamy Peanut Sauce

284 mL	**can Campbell's Condensed Onion Soup**	**10 ounce**
15 mL	**cornstarch**	**1 tablespoon**
15 mL	**soy sauce**	**1 tablespoon**
25 mL	**peanut butter**	**2 tablespoons**
Dash	**cayenne pepper**	**Dash**
25 mL	**peanut or vegetable oil**	**2 tablespoons**
2	**cloves garlic, minced**	**2**
500 g	**boneless beef sirloin steak, cut into very thin strips**	**1 pound**
500 g	**package frozen mixed vegetables**	**16 ounce**
	Chopped peanuts for garnish	

1. In small bowl, stir together soup, cornstarch, soy sauce, peanut butter and cayenne. Set aside.

2. In 3 L (3 quart) microwave-safe casserole, combine 15 mL (1 tablespoon) of the oil and garlic. Cover with lid; microwave on HIGH 1 min.

3. Add beef strips; stir well. Cover; microwave on HIGH 3 min or until beef is no longer pink, stirring once during cooking. Remove beef and garlic from casserole; set aside. Pour off excess liquid.

4. Add remaining 15 mL (1 tablespoon) oil to same casserole. Cover; microwave on HIGH 30 sec. Add vegetables. Cover; microwave on HIGH 4 min or until tender-crisp, stirring once during cooking.

5. Return beef mixture to casserole. Stir soup mixture; stir into casserole. Cover; microwave on HIGH 3 min or until hot. Garnish with peanuts. Makes 4 servings.

■ **TIP**

Use window cleaner to clean interior surfaces of your microwave oven. It will remove odours as well as food splatters.

Campbell's Meat Loaf

500 g	lean ground beef	1 pound
284 mL	can Campbell's Condensed Cream of Mushroom Soup	10 ounce
125 mL	fresh bread crumbs	½ cup
1	egg, beaten	1
Dash	pepper	Dash
125 mL	water	½ cup
10 mL	cornstarch	2 teaspoons
50 mL	chutney	¼ cup
15 mL	chopped pimiento	1 tablespoon
	Chopped fresh parsley for garnish	

1. In large bowl, combine beef, 50 mL (¼ cup) of the soup, bread crumbs, egg and pepper. Press mixture into 22.5 by 12.5 by 7.5 cm (9 by 5 by 3 inch) microwave-safe pan. Cover with waxed paper; microwave at 50% power 22 min, draining liquid occasionally. Let stand 5 min.

2. In small bowl, stir together water and cornstarch. Microwave, uncovered, on HIGH 1 min. Stir in remaining soup and chutney. Cover; microwave on HIGH 3 min or until thickened, stirring once during cooking. Stir in pimiento.

3. Serve sauce with meat loaf. Garnish with parsley. Makes 4 servings.

Barbecue Beef Buns

375 g	beef round steak, 2 cm (¾ inch thick)	¾ pound
25 mL	butter or margarine	2 tablespoons
125 mL	chopped onion	½ cup
1	clove garlic, minced	1
284 mL	can Campbell's Condensed Tomato Soup	10 ounce
25 mL	packed brown sugar	2 tablespoons
25 mL	vinegar	2 tablespoons
10 mL	prepared mustard	2 teaspoons
5 mL	Worcestershire sauce	1 teaspoon
6	hamburger buns, split	6

1. Freeze meat 1 h to make slicing easier. Cut steak across the grain into very thin slices.

2. In 3 L (3 quart) microwave-safe casserole, combine butter, onion and garlic. Cover with lid; microwave on HIGH 2 min.

3. Add meat. Cover; microwave on HIGH 3 min or until meat is no longer pink. Stir in soup, sugar, vinegar, mustard and Worcestershire.

4. Cover; microwave on HIGH 5 min or until hot. Serve on buns. Makes 6 servings.

Zesty Meat Loaf

750 g	lean ground beef	1½ pounds
284 mL	can Campbell's Condensed Tomato Soup	10 ounce
2	eggs, beaten	2
200 mL	finely crushed saltine crackers	¾ cup
25 mL	Worcestershire sauce	2 tablespoons
25 mL	grated Parmesan cheese	2 tablespoons

1. In large bowl, thoroughly mix beef, 125 mL (½ cup) of the soup, eggs, crackers and Worcestershire. In 30 by 20 cm (12 by 8 inch) microwave-safe baking dish, firmly shape meat mixture. Cover with waxed paper; microwave on HIGH 15 min or until loaf is firm in centre, rotating dish twice during cooking.

2. Spread remaining soup over meat. Microwave, uncovered, on HIGH 2 min or until soup is hot. Top with cheese. Let stand, uncovered, 5 min. Makes 6 servings.

NOTE: If you are using a temperature probe, cook meat loaf to an internal temperature of 75°C (170°F).

Picadillo-Stuffed Peppers

4	medium sweet green or red peppers	4
15 mL	water	1 tablespoon
500 g	lean ground beef	1 pound
125 mL	chopped onion	½ cup
1	clove garlic, minced	1
2 mL	ground cinnamon	½ teaspoon
2 mL	ground cumin	½ teaspoon
Dash	ground cloves	Dash
284 mL	can Campbell's Condensed Tomato Soup	10 ounce
1	small apple, cored and chopped	1
50 mL	raisins	¼ cup
50 mL	toasted sliced almonds (see Note on page 98)	¼ cup
15 mL	vinegar	1 tablespoon

1. Cut thin slice from top of each pepper. Chop enough pepper tops to make 75 mL (⅓ cup); set aside. Remove and discard inner membranes and seeds. Place pepper shells in 2 L (2 quart) microwave-safe casserole; add water. Cover with lid; microwave on HIGH 5 min or until tender-crisp. Drain; set aside.

2. Crumble beef into same casserole; add onion, garlic, cinnamon, cumin, cloves and chopped pepper tops. Cover; microwave on HIGH 5 min or until beef is no longer pink, stirring once during cooking to separate meat. Spoon off fat.

3. Stir in remaining ingredients. Divide mixture among peppers. Arrange in 2 L (2 quart) microwave-safe casserole. Cover; microwave on HIGH 5 min or until hot. Makes 4 servings.

Meatball Stew

750 g	ground beef	1½ pounds
1	egg, slightly beaten	1
250 mL	small bread cubes	1 cup
50 mL	finely chopped onion	¼ cup
15 mL	vegetable oil	1 tablespoon
284 mL	can Campbell's Condensed Beef Broth (Bouillon)	10 ounce
284 mL	can Campbell's Condensed Tomato Soup	10 ounce
1 mL	dried thyme leaves, crushed	¼ teaspoon
398 mL	can sliced carrots, drained	14 ounce
540 mL	can whole, white potatoes, drained	19 ounce
398 mL	jar whole onions, drained	14 ounce

1. In large bowl, combine beef, egg, bread cubes and onion. Shape into 24 meatballs. Arrange meatballs in 30 by 20 cm (12 by 8 inch) microwave-safe baking dish. Cover with vented plastic wrap; microwave on HIGH 3 min. Rearrange meatballs. Cover; microwave on HIGH 3 min or until meatballs are no longer pink. Spoon off fat.

2. In medium bowl, combine remaining ingredients. Pour over meatballs. Cover; microwave on HIGH 5 min or until hot, rotating dish once during cooking. Makes 6 servings.

Sloppy Joes

250 mL	chopped onions	1 cup
50 mL	chopped celery	¼ cup
50 mL	chopped green pepper	¼ cup
1	clove garlic, minced	1
25 mL	chili powder	2 tablespoons
500 g	ground beef	1 pound
450 mL	Prego Spaghetti Sauce	1¾ cups
6	hamburger buns or long hard rolls, split and toasted	6

1. In 2 L (2 quart) microwave-safe casserole, combine onions, celery, pepper, garlic and chili powder. Cover with lid; microwave on HIGH 4 min or until vegetables are tender.

2. Add ground beef. Cover; microwave on HIGH 5 min, stirring once during cooking to separate meat. Spoon off fat.

3. Stir in spaghetti sauce. Cover; microwave on HIGH 4 min or until hot. Stir before serving. Serve over toasted buns. Makes 6 sandwiches.

MEATBALL STEW ▶

Chili Rice Casserole

25 mL	**butter or margarine**	**2 tablespoons**
125 mL	**sliced carrot**	**½ cup**
125 mL	**sliced onion**	**½ cup**
1	**large clove garlic, minced**	**1**
5 mL	**chili powder**	**1 teaspoon**
2 mL	**ground cumin**	**½ teaspoon**
375 mL	**cubed cooked ham or beef**	**1½ cups**
250 mL	**regular long-grain rice, uncooked**	**1 cup**
750 mL	**V8 Vegetable Juice**	**3 cups**
	Chopped fresh parsley	

1. In 1.5 L (1½ quart) microwave-safe casserole, combine butter, carrot, onion, garlic, chili powder and cumin. Cover with lid; microwave on HIGH 3 min or until vegetables are tender, stirring once during cooking.

2. Stir in ham, rice and V8 juice. Cover; microwave on HIGH 12 min or until bubbling, stirring once during cooking. Stir again.

3. Reduce power to 50%. Cover; microwave 10 min or until rice is nearly done and liquid is absorbed.

4. Cover with plastic wrap; refrigerate until serving time.

5. Vent plastic wrap; microwave on HIGH 14 min or until hot, stirring once during cooking. Garnish with parsley. Makes 4 servings.

Cheese 'n' Rice-Stuffed Beef Pie

500 g	**lean ground beef**	**1 pound**
1 mL	**salt**	**¼ teaspoon**
125 mL	**fine dry bread crumbs**	**½ cup**
50 mL	**chopped green pepper**	**¼ cup**
50 mL	**chopped onion**	**¼ cup**
250 mL	**quick-cooking rice, uncooked**	**1 cup**
450 mL	**Prego Spaghetti Sauce**	**1¾ cups**
300 mL	**grated Cheddar cheese**	**1¼ cups**

1. In medium bowl, combine beef, salt, crumbs, pepper and onion. Press mixture onto bottom and sides of 22.5 cm (9 inch) microwave-safe pie plate, forming a crust; set aside.

2. In medium bowl, combine rice, spaghetti sauce and 250 mL (1 cup) of the cheese. Spoon mixture into beef crust.

3. Cover with vented plastic wrap. Microwave on HIGH 10 min. Carefully spoon off fat. Sprinkle with remaining cheese. Let stand 5 min. Makes 6 servings.

Spicy Chili Verde

Serve this flavourful stew with chili beans for an authentic Western meal.

750 g	**pork for stew, cut into 1.5 cm (½ inch) pieces**	**1½ pounds**
75 mL	**all-purpose flour**	**⅓ cup**
200 mL	**chopped green pepper**	**¾ cup**
125 mL	**chopped onion**	**½ cup**
284 mL	**can Campbell's Condensed Tomato Soup**	**10 ounce**
284 mL	**can Campbell's Condensed Beef Consommé**	**10 ounce**
250 mL	**water**	**1 cup**
25 mL	**drained, canned chopped green chilies**	**2 tablespoons**
15 mL	**lemon juice**	**1 tablespoon**
2	**cloves garlic, minced**	**2**
1	**bay leaf**	**1**
5 mL	**dried oregano leaves, crushed**	**1 teaspoon**
1 mL	**ground cumin**	**¼ teaspoon**
Dash	**hot pepper sauce**	**Dash**
Dash	**ground cloves**	**Dash**
	Hot cooked rice	

1. Coat pork in flour. In 3 L (3 quart) microwave-safe casserole, combine pork, green pepper and onion. Cover with lid; microwave on HIGH 8 min, stirring once during cooking.

2. Stir in soup, consommé, water, chilies, lemon juice, garlic, bay leaf, oregano, cumin, hot pepper sauce and cloves. Cover; microwave on HIGH 8 min or until bubbling, stirring once during cooking.

3. Reduce power to 50%. Cover; microwave 45 min or until pork is no longer pink, stirring 3 times during cooking. Let stand, covered, 5 min. Remove bay leaf. Serve over rice. Makes 6 servings.

■ **TIP**

When it comes to cooking rice, the microwave oven won't save you cooking time. However, it will make cleanup easier because the rice won't stick to the pan. For hot cooked rice, combine equal parts quick-cooking rice and water in a glass measure. Cover with vented plastic wrap. Cook on HIGH until boiling. For 1 serving or ¼ cup uncooked quick-cooking rice, allow 1 minute. For 4 servings or 1¼ cups uncooked quick-cooking rice, allow 3 minutes. Let stand, covered, 5 minutes.

Chili Burritos

This zesty filling mixture also makes hearty sandwiches when served on hamburger rolls.

500 g	**ground beef**	**1 pound**
50 mL	**chopped green pepper**	**¼ cup**
284 mL	**can Campbell's Condensed Tomato Soup**	**10 ounce**
15 mL	**chili powder**	**1 tablespoon**
25 mL	**Worcestershire sauce**	**2 tablespoons**
8 (20 cm)	**flour tortillas**	**8 (8 inch)**
	Guacamole for garnish	
	Chopped tomatoes for garnish	
	Grated Cheddar cheese for garnish	

1. Crumble beef into 2 L (2 quart) microwave-safe casserole; stir in pepper. Cover with lid; microwave on HIGH 5 min or until beef is no longer pink, stirring once during cooking to break up meat. Spoon off fat.

2. Stir in soup, chili powder and Worcestershire. Cover; microwave on HIGH 5 min or until hot and bubbling.

3. Wrap stack of tortillas in damp paper towels. Microwave on HIGH 1 min or until warm. Spoon heaping 50 mL (¼ cup) meat mixture onto each tortilla. Fold in sides and roll up to make burritos. Garnish with guacamole, tomatoes and cheese. Makes 4 servings.

Smothered Liver and Onions

25 mL	**butter or margarine**	**2 tablespoons**
1	**large onion, thinly sliced**	**1**
500 g	**beef liver, 1 cm (¼ inch) thick**	**1 pound**
284 mL	**can Campbell's Condensed Cream of Mushroom Soup**	**10 ounce**
50 mL	**milk or half-and-half**	**¼ cup**
Dash	**pepper**	**Dash**

1. In 30 by 20 cm (12 by 8 inch) microwave-safe baking dish, combine butter and onion. Cover with vented plastic wrap; microwave on HIGH 5 min or until onion is tender, stirring once during cooking.

2. Cut liver into 4 portions. Arrange liver over onions, placing thicker portions toward edges of dish. In small bowl, stir soup until smooth; stir in milk and pepper. Pour over liver. Cover; microwave on HIGH 10 min or until liver is no longer pink, rearranging liver twice during cooking. Let stand, covered, 5 min. Makes 4 servings.

CHILI BURRITOS ▶

Down Home Hash and Eggs

25 mL	butter or margarine	2 tablespoons
1 L	diced, cooked and peeled potatoes	4 cups
284 mL	can Campbell's Condensed Cream of Celery Soup	10 ounce
50 mL	milk	¼ cup
15 mL	Dijon-style mustard	1 tablespoon
1 mL	hot pepper sauce	¼ teaspoon
375 mL	chopped cooked corned beef	1½ cups
4	eggs	4
	Chopped fresh parsley for garnish	

1. In 2 L (2 quart) microwave-safe casserole, combine butter and potatoes. Cover with lid; microwave on HIGH 3 min, stirring once during cooking.

2. Stir in soup, milk, mustard and hot pepper sauce. Cover; microwave on HIGH 3 min or until edges are hot and bubbling, stirring once during cooking. Stir in corned beef.

3. Make 4 indentations in potato mixture. Gently break 1 egg into each indentation. With toothpick, pierce each yolk. Cover; microwave at 50% power 8 min or until eggs are almost set, rotating dish once during cooking. Let stand, covered, 2 min. Garnish with parsley. Makes 4 servings.

Garden-Style Ravioli

75 mL	olive oil	⅓ cup
375 mL	carrots cut into 4 cm (1½ inch) julienne strips	1½ cups
375 mL	green pepper cut into 4 cm (1½ inch) julienne strips	1½ cups
375 mL	zucchini cut into 4 cm (1½ inch) julienne strips	1½ cups
1.25 L	Prego Spaghetti Sauce	5 cups
36	frozen cheese- or meat-filled ravioli, cooked and drained	36

1. In 3 L (3 quart) microwave-safe casserole, combine oil, carrots, pepper and zucchini. Cover with lid; microwave on HIGH 5 min or until vegetables are tender-crisp.

2. Stir in spaghetti sauce. Cover; microwave on HIGH 5 min or until hot. Stir before serving. Serve over ravioli. Makes 6 servings.

Sweet and Sour Pork

500 g	**boneless pork, cut into 2.5 cm (1 inch) pieces**	**1 pound**
1	**clove garlic, minced**	**1**
284 mL	**can Campbell's Condensed Beef Consommé**	**10 ounce**
25 mL	**packed brown sugar**	**2 tablespoons**
25 mL	**vinegar**	**2 tablespoons**
1	**sweet green pepper, cut into strips**	**1**
1	**sweet red pepper, cut into strips**	**1**
50 mL	**cornstarch**	**¼ cup**
25 mL	**soy sauce**	**2 tablespoons**
540 mL	**can pineapple chunks, drained**	**19 ounce**
	Hot cooked rice	

1. In 2 L (2 quart) microwave-safe casserole, combine pork and garlic. Cover with lid; microwave on HIGH 6 min or until pork is no longer pink, stirring once. Spoon off fat. Stir in consommé, sugar, vinegar and peppers. Cover; microwave on HIGH 5 min or until bubbling, stirring twice during cooking.

2. In small bowl, stir together cornstarch and soy sauce; stir into casserole. Stir in pineapple. Cover; microwave on HIGH 3 min or until thickened, stirring once. Let stand, covered, 3 min. Serve over rice. Makes 5 servings.

Shanghai Pork

500 g	**boneless pork, cut into 2.5 cm (1 inch) cubes**	**1 pound**
2	**cloves garlic, minced**	**2**
2 mL	**grated orange peel**	**½ teaspoon**
25 mL	**cornstarch**	**2 tablespoons**
75 mL	**water**	**⅓ cup**
284 mL	**can Campbell's Condensed Beef Broth (Bouillon)**	**10 ounce**
5 mL	**ground ginger**	**1 teaspoon**
250 mL	**carrots sliced 1.5 cm (½ inch) thick**	**1 cup**
250 mL	**sweet red and green peppers cut into 4 cm (1½ inch) strips**	**1 cup**
	Hot cooked rice (optional)	

1. In 3 L (3 quart) microwave-safe casserole, combine pork, garlic and orange peel. Cover with lid; microwave on HIGH 7 min or until pork is no longer pink, stirring once during cooking. Spoon off fat.

2. In small bowl, stir together cornstarch and water. Stir into pork mixture. Stir in broth, ginger, carrots and peppers. Cover; microwave on HIGH 9 min or until vegetables are tender, stirring once during cooking. Serve with rice if desired. Makes 4 servings.

Oriental Pork

5 mL	**sesame oil**	**1 teaspoon**
5 mL	**vegetable oil**	**1 teaspoon**
5 mL	**grated fresh ginger**	**1 teaspoon**
15 mL	**soy sauce**	**1 tablespoon**
15 mL	**dry sherry**	**1 tablespoon**
1	**clove garlic, minced**	**1**
500 g	**boneless pork, cut into 5 by 1 cm (2 by ¼ inch) strips**	**1 pound**
284 mL	**can Campbell's Condensed Beef Broth (Bouillon)**	**10 ounce**
25 mL	**cornstarch**	**2 tablespoons**
250 mL	**snow peas, cleaned**	**1 cup**
1	**sweet red pepper, cut into strips**	**1**
250 mL	**sliced fresh mushrooms**	**1 cup**
	Hot cooked rice	

1. In 3 L (3 quart) microwave-safe casserole, combine oils, ginger, soy sauce, sherry and garlic. Add pork; toss to coat. Cover with lid; refrigerate 1 h.

2. Microwave, covered, on HIGH 5 min or until pork is no longer pink, stirring once during cooking.

3. In small bowl, combine broth and cornstarch; stir into pork mixture. Stir in peas, pepper and mushrooms. Cover; microwave on HIGH 7 min or until hot and bubbling, stirring 3 times during cooking. Serve over rice. Makes 5 servings.

■ **TIP**

It's important to cook pork thoroughly. Because microwave ovens may heat unevenly, you'll need to take special care when cooking pork. Follow these simple guidelines and you'll be pleased with the tender, juicy and thoroughly cooked results.

• Cook pork covered with either a tight-fitting lid or vented plastic wrap. The cover traps the cooking steam, which helps to distribute heat more evenly in the dish.

• At the end of cooking, check for doneness by cutting into several large pieces of pork. Pork is cooked when the juices are clear, the meat is no longer pink and the internal temperature is 77°C (170°F). If the pork is undercooked, continue cooking and check doneness frequently.

ORIENTAL PORK ▶

Asparagus-Ham Roll-Ups

500 g	**fresh asparagus**	**1 pound**
25 mL	**water**	**2 tablespoons**
8 (28 g)	**slices boiled ham**	**8 (1 ounce)**
284 mL	**can Campbell's Condensed Cream of Celery Soup**	**10 ounce**
125 mL	**sour cream**	**½ cup**
50 mL	**milk**	**¼ cup**
25 mL	**chopped fresh parsley**	**2 tablespoons**
5 mL	**prepared mustard**	**1 teaspoon**
	Hot cooked rice	

1. Arrange asparagus with tips toward centre in 30 by 20 cm (12 by 8 inch) microwave-safe baking dish; add water. Cover with vented plastic wrap; microwave on HIGH 4 min or until asparagus is tender, rotating dish once during cooking. Drain well.

2. Divide asparagus spears among ham slices; roll ham around asparagus. Secure with wooden toothpicks if necessary. Arrange rolls in same baking dish.

3. In small bowl, stir soup until smooth. Stir in sour cream, milk, parsley and mustard. Pour over ham rolls. Cover with vented plastic wrap; microwave at 50% power 13 min or until hot. Let stand, covered, 5 min. Serve over rice. Makes 4 servings.

NOTE: Substitute one 284 g (10 ounce) package frozen asparagus spears for fresh asparagus. Cook according to package directions. Drain well, then proceed as above in steps 2 and 3.

Ham-Sauced Sweet Potatoes

3 (250 g)	**sweet potatoes**	**3 (8 ounce)**
284 mL	**can Campbell's Condensed Cream of Mushroom Soup**	**10 ounce**
250 mL	**cooked ham cut into thin strips**	**1 cup**
2 mL	**grated orange peel**	**½ teaspoon**
75 mL	**orange juice**	**⅓ cup**
50 mL	**raisins**	**¼ cup**

1. With fork, pierce potatoes in several places; arrange in circular pattern on microwave-safe plate. Microwave, uncovered, on HIGH 8 min or until tender, rearranging potatoes once during cooking. Let stand, uncovered, while preparing sauce.

2. In 1.5 L (1½ quart) microwave-safe casserole, combine remaining ingredients. Cover with lid; microwave on HIGH 4 min or until hot, stirring once during cooking. Split potatoes; spoon sauce over each. Makes 3 servings.

Ham Meatballs

375 g	**ground ham**	**¾ pound**
375 g	**ground pork**	**¾ pound**
125 mL	**fine dry bread crumbs, seasoned**	**½ cup**
1	**egg**	**1**
284 mL	**can Campbell's Condensed Tomato Soup**	**10 ounce**
125 mL	**packed brown sugar**	**½ cup**
50 mL	**vinegar**	**¼ cup**
2 mL	**dry mustard**	**½ teaspoon**

1. In medium bowl, thoroughly combine ham, pork, bread crumbs and egg. Shape mixture into 2.5 cm (1 inch) meatballs. Arrange in single layer in 30 by 20 cm (12 by 8 inch) microwave-safe baking dish. Cover with vented plastic wrap; microwave on HIGH 8 min or until meatballs are firm, rearranging meatballs once during cooking. Spoon off fat. Let stand, covered, while preparing sauce.

2. In 1 L (4 cup) glass measure, combine remaining ingredients. Microwave, uncovered, on HIGH 3 min or until bubbling, stirring once during cooking.

3. Pour sauce over meatballs. Cover; microwave on HIGH 3 min or until heated through. Makes 48 meatballs.

NOTE: If you don't see ground ham in your supermarket, ask the butcher to grind it for you or finely chop cubed, cooked ham in a food processor.

■ **TIP**

Here's an easy way to shape meatballs so they're all the same size for even cooking. On waxed paper, pat meat mixture out to a 2.5 cm (1 inch) thick square. With a large knife, cut meat into desired number of squares, then roll each square in your hands to form a meatball.

Lamb Stew

750 g	boneless lamb, cut into 1.5 cm (½ inch) pieces	1½ pounds
284 mL	can Franco-American Mushroom Gravy	10 ounce
4	small potatoes, quartered	4
5 mL	dried mint leaves, crushed	1 teaspoon
250 mL	frozen peas	1 cup
250 mL	quartered fresh mushrooms	1 cup
15 mL	lemon juice	1 tablespoon

1. Place lamb in 3 L (3 quart) microwave-safe casserole. Cover with lid; microwave on HIGH 6 min or until lamb is no longer pink, stirring once during cooking. Spoon off fat.

2. Stir in gravy, potatoes and mint. Cover; microwave on HIGH 5 min or until bubbling. Stir again. Reduce power to 50%. Cover; microwave 20 min or until meat is almost tender, stirring twice during cooking.

3. Stir in peas, mushrooms and lemon juice. Cover; microwave at 50% power 10 min or until vegetables and meat are tender, stirring once during cooking. Let stand, covered, 5 min. Makes 6 servings.

Lamb-Stuffed Eggplant

2	medium eggplants, about 500 g (1 pound) each	2
50 mL	chopped carrot	¼ cup
1	clove garlic, minced	1
5 to 7 mL	dried mint leaves, crushed	1 to 1½ teaspoons
250 g	ground lamb	½ pound
284 mL	can Campbell's Condensed Tomato Soup	10 ounce
250 mL	cooked rice	1 cup
25 mL	chopped fresh parsley	2 tablespoons
5 mL	lemon juice	1 teaspoon

1. Cut each eggplant in half lengthwise; scoop out pulp, leaving 1 cm (¼ inch) shell. Cube pulp. In 2 L (2 quart) microwave-safe casserole, combine cubed eggplant, carrot, garlic and mint. Cover with lid; microwave on HIGH 3 min.

2. Stir in lamb. Cover; microwave on HIGH 3 min or until lamb is no longer pink, stirring once to separate meat. Stir in soup, rice, parsley and lemon juice. Spoon into eggplant shells. Arrange in 30 by 20 cm (12 by 8 inch) microwave-safe baking dish. Cover with vented plastic wrap; microwave on HIGH 11 min or until eggplant is tender, rearranging eggplant halves once. Let stand, covered, 2 min. Makes 4 servings.

NOTE: Ground beef can be used in place of the ground lamb.

Lamb Curry

15 mL	**butter or margarine**	**1 tablespoon**
250 mL	**chopped onion**	**1 cup**
25 mL	**curry powder**	**2 tablespoons**
750 g	**boneless lamb, cut into 1.5 cm (½ inch) pieces**	**1½ pounds**
50 mL	**all-purpose flour**	**¼ cup**
284 mL	**can Campbell's Condensed Chicken Broth**	**10 ounce**
2	**apples, peeled, cored and chopped**	**2**
455 mL	**can tomatoes, drained and chopped (optional)**	**16 ounce**
50 mL	**chutney**	**¼ cup**
125 mL	**sour cream or plain yogurt**	**½ cup**
	Hot cooked rice	
	Chopped peanuts for garnish	

1. In 3 L (3 quart) microwave-safe casserole, combine butter, onion and curry powder. Cover with lid; microwave on HIGH 4 min or until onion is tender, stirring once during cooking.

2. In large bowl, toss lamb with flour. Stir into casserole. Cover; microwave on HIGH 6 min or until meat is no longer pink, stirring once during cooking.

3. Stir in broth, apples, tomatoes and chutney. Cover; microwave on HIGH 7 min or until bubbling, stirring once during cooking. Stir again. Reduce power to 50%. Microwave 30 min or until meat is tender, stirring 3 times during cooking. Let stand, covered, 5 min. Stir in sour cream. Serve over rice. Garnish with peanuts. Makes 6 servings.

Veal Stew

500 g	**veal for stew, cut into 1.5 cm (½ inch) pieces**	**1 pound**
15 mL	**all-purpose flour**	**1 tablespoon**
284 mL	**can Campbell's Gold Label Cream of Mushroom Soup**	**10 ounce**
250 mL	**frozen baby carrots**	**1 cup**
	OR	
	fresh carrots cut into sticks	
125 mL	**pearl onions, peeled**	**½ cup**
1 mL	**dried thyme leaves, crushed**	**¼ teaspoon**
5 mL	**lemon juice**	**1 teaspoon**

1. In 2 L (2 quart) microwave-safe casserole, toss veal with flour. Cover with lid; microwave on HIGH 5 min or until veal is no longer pink, stirring once.

2. Stir soup into meat until smooth. Stir in carrots, onions and thyme. Cover; microwave at 50% power 25 min or until veal is tender, stirring 3 times during cooking. Stir in lemon juice. Let stand, covered, 5 min. Makes 4 servings.

Lasagna

250 g	Italian sausage, casing removed	½ pound
250 mL	chopped onion	1 cup
1 L	Prego Spaghetti Sauce	4 cups
500 g	ricotta cheese	16 ounces
250 mL	grated mozzarella cheese	1 cup
2	eggs, beaten	2
9	lasagna noodles, cooked and drained	9
50 mL	grated Parmesan cheese	¼ cup

1. Crumble sausage into 2 L (2 quart) microwave-safe casserole; stir in onion. Cover with lid; microwave on HIGH 5 min or until sausage is no longer pink, stirring once to separate meat. Spoon off fat. Stir in spaghetti sauce. Cover; microwave on HIGH 5 min or until hot.

2. Meanwhile, in small bowl, combine ricotta, mozzarella and eggs. Spread 250 mL (1 cup) of the sauce mixture in 30 by 20 cm (12 by 8 inch) microwave-safe baking dish. Top with 3 lasagna noodles, ½ of the cheese mixture and 250 mL (1 cup) of the sauce. Repeat layers, ending with 3 noodles and remaining sauce.

3. Cover with vented plastic wrap; microwave at 50% power 30 min or until hot and bubbling, rotating dish twice during cooking. Sprinkle with Parmesan cheese. Let stand, covered, 15 min. Makes 8 servings.

Stuffed Cabbage

6	cabbage leaves	6
125 mL	water	½ cup
500 g	ground beef or pork	1 pound
250 mL	cooked rice	1 cup
125 mL	chopped onion	½ cup
1	egg	1
15 mL	Worcestershire sauce	1 tablespoon
Dash	pepper	Dash
284 mL	can Campbell's Condensed Tomato Soup	10 ounce
10 mL	vinegar	2 teaspoons

1. Arrange cabbage leaves in 3 L (3 quart) microwave-safe casserole; add water. Cover with lid; microwave on HIGH 6 min or until soft, rotating dish once during cooking. Drain and set aside.

2. In medium bowl, thoroughly mix beef, rice, onion, egg, Worcestershire, pepper and 25 mL (2 tablespoons) of the soup. Lay drained cabbage leaves on counter. Spoon about 125 mL (½ cup) of the meat mixture onto each leaf. Fold in sides and roll up to form bundles; secure with wooden toothpicks if necessary. Arrange in same casserole.

3. In small bowl, combine remaining soup and vinegar. Spoon over cabbage rolls. Cover; microwave on HIGH 15 min or until meat is cooked, rotating dish once during cooking. Let stand, covered, 5 min. Makes 6 servings.

Spaghetti Squash Lasagna

500 g	**ground beef**	**1 pound**
250 g	**hot Italian sausage, casing removed**	**½ pound**
1 L	**Prego Spaghetti Sauce**	**4 cups**
500 mL	**ricotta cheese**	**2 cups**
625 mL	**cooked spaghetti squash**	**2½ cups**
1	**egg, slightly beaten**	**1**
125 mL	**grated Parmesan cheese**	**½ cup**
9	**lasagna noodles, cooked and drained**	**9**

1. Crumble beef and sausage into 2 L (2 quart) microwave-safe casserole. Cover with lid; microwave on HIGH 6 min or until meat is no longer pink, stirring once during cooking to separate meat. Spoon off fat.

2. Stir in spaghetti sauce. Cover; microwave on HIGH 3 min or until hot, stirring once during cooking.

3. Meanwhile, in medium bowl, combine ricotta cheese, 500 mL (2 cups) of the spaghetti squash, egg and 50 mL (¼ cup) of the Parmesan cheese.

4. Spread 375 mL (1½ cups) of the sauce in 30 by 20 cm (12 by 8 inch) microwave-safe baking dish. Arrange 3 lasagna noodles, ½ of the cheese mixture and 200 mL (¾ cup) of the sauce. Repeat layers. Top with remaining noodles, sauce, squash and Parmesan cheese. Cover with plastic wrap; refrigerate until serving time.

5. Vent plastic wrap; microwave on HIGH 5 min. Rotate dish. Reduce power to 50%; microwave 20 min or until hot. Let stand, covered, 5 min. Makes 4 servings.

■ **TIP**

If you're saving leftovers in the freezer for reheating in the microwave, freeze them in single-serving portions. You can remove exactly the number of portions you need. They'll reheat more quickly and evenly than portions frozen together. Put 3 or 4 small portions in sandwich bags then place the small bags in a large freezer bag.

Sausage and Potatoes Italiano

For a milder flavour, substitute 500 g (1 pound) of ground beef for the sausage.

500 g	**hot Italian sausage, casing removed**	**1 pound**
125 mL	**chopped onion**	**½ cup**
1 L	**thinly sliced potatoes**	**4 cups**
450 mL	**Prego Spaghetti Sauce**	**1¾ cups**
1 mL	**pepper**	**¼ teaspoon**
250 mL	**grated mozzarella cheese**	**1 cup**

1. Crumble sausage into 2 L (2 quart) microwave-safe casserole; stir in onion. Cover with lid; microwave on HIGH 5 min or until sausage is no longer pink; stirring once during cooking to separate meat. Spoon off fat.

2. Stir in potatoes, spaghetti sauce and pepper. Cover; microwave on HIGH 20 min or until potatoes are tender, stirring once during cooking. Sprinkle with cheese. Let stand, uncovered, 5 min. Makes 4 servings.

Warm Sausage and Potato Salad

Serve this warm, hearty dish on a bed of greens and call it a salad, or serve it from the cooking dish and call it a casserole.

284 mL	**can Franco-American Chicken Gravy**	**10 ounce**
4	**green onions, sliced**	**4**
25 mL	**wine vinegar**	**2 tablespoons**
15 mL	**Dijon-style mustard**	**1 tablespoon**
750 g	**small potatoes, cut into 1 cm (¼ inch) slices**	**1½ pounds**
250 g	**kielbasa or other smoked sausage diced**	**½ pound**
25 mL	**chopped fresh parsley**	**2 tablespoons**

1. In 3 L (3 quart) microwave-safe casserole, combine gravy, onions, vinegar and mustard. Stir in potatoes and sausage.

2. Cover with lid; microwave on HIGH 25 min or until potatoes are tender, stirring twice during cooking. Let stand, covered, 5 min. Sprinkle with parsley. Makes 4 servings.

Sausage and Pepper Polenta

500 g	**Italian sausage, casing removed**	**1 pound**
1	**sweet red pepper, cut into strips**	**1**
1	**sweet green pepper, cut into strips**	**1**
1	**large onion, thinly sliced**	**1**
2	**cloves garlic, minced**	**2**
450 mL	**Prego Spaghetti Sauce**	**1¾ cups**
125 mL	**yellow cornmeal**	**½ cup**
5 mL	**olive or vegetable oil**	**1 teaspoon**
500 mL	**water**	**2 cups**
75 mL	**grated Parmesan cheese**	**⅓ cup**

1. Crumble sausage into 20 by 20 cm (8 by 8 inch) microwave-safe baking dish. Stir in peppers, onion and garlic. Cover with vented plastic wrap; microwave on HIGH 10 min or until sausage is no longer pink, stirring twice during cooking to separate meat. Spoon off fat. Stir spaghetti sauce into sausage mixture; set aside.

2. In 2 L (2 quart) microwave-safe casserole, combine cornmeal and oil. Stir in water. Cover with lid; microwave on HIGH 8 min or until very thick, stirring 3 times during cooking.

3. Spread over sausage mixture. Cover with vented plastic wrap; microwave at 50% power 7 min or until very hot. Sprinkle with cheese. Let stand, covered, 10 min. Makes 6 servings.

Sausage Sandwiches: Omit cornmeal, oil, water and Parmesan. Prepare as above in step 1. Cover; microwave on HIGH 3 min or until hot and bubbling, stirring once during cooking. Spoon over 4 split hard rolls. Makes 4 sandwiches.

■ **TIP**

Cook ground beef or bulk sausage in a microwave-safe colander set in a larger bowl or casserole. The fat will drain off the meat during cooking.

Eggs and Cheese

Italian Mushroom Omelet

50 mL	**butter or margarine**	**¼ cup**
750 mL	**sliced fresh mushrooms**	**3 cups**
25 mL	**chopped green pepper**	**2 tablespoons**
450 mL	**Prego Spaghetti Sauce**	**1¾ cups**
25 mL	**sliced pitted ripe olives**	**2 tablespoons**
8	**eggs**	**8**
125 mL	**milk**	**½ cup**
Dash	**salt**	**Dash**
125 mL	**grated Cheddar cheese**	**½ cup**

1. In 1.5 L (1½ quart) microwave-safe casserole, combine 15 mL (1 tablespoon) butter, mushrooms and pepper. Cover with lid; microwave on HIGH 3 min or until vegetables are tender, stirring once during cooking.

2. Stir in spaghetti sauce and olives. Cover; microwave on HIGH 3 min or until hot and bubbling. Stir; set aside.

3. Pour ½ of the remaining butter in 22.5 cm (9 inch) microwave-safe pie plate. Cover with waxed paper; microwave on HIGH 20 sec or until melted. Brush onto pie plate.

4. In medium bowl, combine eggs, milk and salt. Pour ½ of the egg mixture into pie plate. Cover; microwave on HIGH 2 min. With spatula, gently move cooked outer edge of omelet to centre, letting uncooked portion flow to edge. Cover; microwave on HIGH 2 min or until centre is set. Transfer omelet to serving plate.

5. Repeat steps 3 and 4 with remaining butter and egg mixture. Spoon about 125 mL (½ cup) of the sauce in centre of each omelet; fold omelet in half. Top with more sauce and cheese. Serve with remaining sauce. Makes 4 servings.

ITALIAN MUSHROOM OMELET ▶

Apple-Cheddar Omelet

4	**slices bacon, chopped**	**4**
284 mL	**can Campbell's Condensed Cheddar Cheese Soup**	**10 ounce**
8	**eggs**	**8**
75 mL	**milk**	**⅓ cup**
1	**small apple, peeled, cored and chopped**	**1**
250 mL	**grated Cheddar cheese**	**1 cup**
Dash	**pepper**	**Dash**

1. Place bacon in 22.5 cm (9 inch) microwave-safe pie plate. Cover with paper towel; microwave on HIGH 3 min or until crisp, stirring once during cooking. Transfer bacon to paper towels. Reserve drippings.

2. In medium bowl, stir ½ of the soup until smooth. Add eggs; beat until well blended. Set aside.

3. To make sauce: In 1 L (1 quart) microwave-safe casserole, stir remaining soup until smooth. Stir in milk, apple, cheese and pepper. Cover with lid; microwave on HIGH 4 min or until hot and bubbling, stirring once during cooking. Let stand while preparing omelets.

4. Brush 5 mL (1 teaspoon) of the bacon drippings onto bottom and sides of same pie plate. Pour in ½ of the egg mixture. Cover with waxed paper; microwave on HIGH 2 min. With spatula, gently move cooked outer edge of omelet toward centre, allowing uncooked portions to flow toward edge. Cover; microwave on HIGH 2 min or until centre is set. Fold omelet in half; slide onto serving plate.

5. Repeat step 4 with 5 mL (1 teaspoon) of the bacon drippings and remaining egg mixture. Spoon sauce over each omelet; sprinkle with bacon. Makes 4 servings.

■ **TIP**

Frozen bagels and English muffins make better toast when they're thawed before toasting. On paper towels, place frozen halves side by side; microwave on HIGH 15 sec.

Huevos Rancheros

15 mL	**vegetable oil**	**1 tablespoon**
50 mL	**chopped green pepper**	**¼ cup**
50 mL	**chopped onion**	**¼ cup**
10 mL	**chili powder**	**2 teaspoons**
284 mL	**can Campbell's Condensed Tomato Soup**	**10 ounce**
50 mL	**water**	**¼ cup**
4	**eggs**	**4**
4 (15 cm)	**corn tortillas**	**4 (6 inch)**
50 mL	**grated Cheddar cheese**	**¼ cup**
	Chopped fresh parsley for garnish	

1. In 2 L (2 quart) microwave-safe casserole, combine oil, pepper, onion and chili powder. Cover with lid; microwave on HIGH 3 min or until vegetables are tender, stirring once during cooking.

2. Stir in soup and water. Cover; microwave on HIGH 5 min or until edges are hot and bubbling, stirring once during cooking.

3. Gently break each egg, sliding onto soup mixture and arranging around edge of casserole. With toothpick, pierce each egg yolk. Cover; microwave at 50% power 4 min or until eggs are almost set, rotating dish once during cooking. Let stand, covered, 2 min.

4. Meanwhile, wrap stack of tortillas in damp paper towels. Microwave on HIGH 30 sec or until warm.

5. Spoon 1 egg and some sauce onto each tortilla. Sprinkle 15 mL (1 tablespoon) of the cheese over each egg. Garnish with parsley. Makes 4 servings.

■ TIP

Don't attempt to hard-cook eggs in the shell in the microwave oven; they will explode. For a quick substitution for chopped hard-cooked egg, simply scramble an egg in the microwave oven, then chop. To prepare: In small microwave-safe bowl, beat 1 egg until frothy. Cover with waxed paper; microwave on HIGH 1 min or until egg is firm, stirring once during cooking. The fluffy texture is different than a hard-cooked egg, but works well in many dishes.

Campbelled Eggs

Nacho Cheese Soup brings a great new taste to this classic recipe.

284 mL	**can Campbell's Condensed Nacho Cheese, Cream of Chicken or Cream of Mushroom Soup**	**10 ounce**
8	**eggs**	**8**
	Chopped fresh parsley for garnish	

1. In 3 L (3 quart) microwave-safe casserole, stir soup until smooth. Add eggs; beat until smooth.

2. Cover with lid; microwave on HIGH 6 min or until eggs are nearly set, stirring 3 times during cooking. Let stand, covered, 2 min. Garnish with parsley. Makes 4 servings.

Broccoli-Cheese Pie

284 mL	**can Campbell's Condensed Cheddar Cheese Soup**	**10 ounce**
375 mL	**cooked rice**	**1½ cups**
4	**eggs**	**4**
284 g	**package frozen chopped broccoli, cooked and drained**	**10 ounce**
250 mL	**ricotta or creamed cottage cheese**	**1 cup**
1	**sweet red pepper, cut into julienne strips**	**1**
1 mL	**black pepper**	**¼ teaspoon**

1. In medium bowl, stir ⅓ of the soup until smooth; stir in rice and 1 of the eggs. Press mixture onto bottom and sides of 22.5 cm (9 inch) microwave-safe pie plate, forming a crust. Microwave, uncovered, on HIGH 2 min or until almost set. Let stand while preparing filling.

2. In large bowl, stir remaining soup until smooth. Stir in remaining 3 eggs and remaining ingredients. Spoon into rice crust.

3. Microwave, uncovered, at 50% power 22 min or until centre is set, rotating dish 3 times during cooking. Let stand, uncovered, 10 min. Makes 6 servings.

Tortellini in Cream Sauce

125 mL	**chopped sweet red pepper**	**½ cup**
50 mL	**chopped onion**	**¼ cup**
2	**cloves garlic, minced**	**2**
5 mL	**olive or vegetable oil**	**1 teaspoon**
284 mL	**can Campbell's Condensed Cream of Mushroom Soup**	**10 ounce**
125 mL	**half-and-half or milk**	**½ cup**
50 mL	**Chablis or other dry white wine**	**¼ cup**
1 mL	**dried tarragon leaves, crushed**	**¼ teaspoon**
250 g	**cheese-filled tortellini, cooked and drained**	**8 ounces**
125 mL	**crumbled Feta or grated Parmesan cheese**	**½ cup**
50 mL	**sliced green onions**	**¼ cup**

1. In 2 L (2 quart) microwave-safe casserole, combine pepper, chopped onion, garlic and oil. Cover with lid; microwave on HIGH 2 min or until vegetables are tender, stirring once during cooking.

2. Stir in soup until smooth. Stir in half-and-half, Chablis and tarragon. Cover; microwave on HIGH 5 min or until hot and bubbling, stirring once during cooking. Let stand, covered, 5 min.

3. Toss with hot tortellini. Sprinkle with cheese and green onions. Makes 4 servings.

■ **TIP**

Summertime is one of the best reasons to own a microwave oven, because the kitchen will stay cool while you cook. Since microwave ovens heat only the food (unlike the conventional oven), the only heat that warms the air comes directly from the food.

Spinach-Tofu Lasagna

450 mL	**Prego Spaghetti Sauce**	**1¾ cups**
500 g	**tofu, well drained**	**1 pound**
2	**eggs**	**2**
125 mL	**ricotta cheese**	**½ cup**
125 mL	**grated Parmesan cheese**	**½ cup**
284 g	**package frozen chopped spinach, thawed and well drained (see Note on page 34)**	**10 ounce**
2 mL	**Italian seasoning, crushed**	**½ teaspoon**
Dash	**pepper**	**Dash**
6	**lasagna noodles, cooked and drained**	**6**
500 mL	**grated mozzarella cheese**	**2 cups**

1. Heat spaghetti sauce according to label directions. Set aside.

2. Meanwhile, in large bowl, mash tofu. Stir in eggs, ricotta, 75 mL (⅓ cup) of the Parmesan, spinach, Italian seasoning and pepper.

3. Spread 25 mL (2 tablespoons) of the spaghetti sauce in 20 by 20 cm (8 by 8 inch) microwave-safe baking dish. Fit 2 noodles into baking dish, cutting and piecing as needed. Layer ⅓ of the remaining sauce, ½ of the tofu mixture and ½ of the mozzarella over the noodles. Repeat layers of 2 noodles, ⅓ of the sauce, remaining tofu mixture and remaining mozzarella. Top with remaining 2 noodles, remaining sauce and remaining Parmesan.

4. Cover with vented plastic wrap; microwave on HIGH 8 min or until hot. Rotate dish. Reduce power to 50%. Microwave, covered, 12 min or until hot and bubbling, rotating dish twice during cooking. Let stand, covered, 5 min. Makes 6 servings.

■ **TIP**

For quick microwave oven cleanup, heat about 125 mL (½ cup) water to boiling in the oven. The steam will help any cooked-on food come off more easily.

Eggplant Parmesan

This microwave method helps you avoid extra calories. Most conventional eggplant recipes require oil for frying or broiling, but you don't need any here.

1	**egg**	**1**
25 mL	**milk**	**2 tablespoons**
250 mL	**Italian-seasoned fine dry bread crumbs**	**1 cup**
1	**medium eggplant, peeled and cut into 1 cm (¼ inch) slices**	**1**
450 mL	**Prego Spaghetti Sauce**	**1¾ cups**
500 mL	**grated mozzarella cheese**	**2 cups**
25 mL	**grated Parmesan cheese**	**2 tablespoons**

1. In pie plate, beat egg and milk. Place crumbs in another pie plate. Dip eggplant slices into egg mixture, then into crumbs to coat well.

2. Arrange ½ of the eggplant slices on 25 cm (10 inch) microwave-safe plate lined with paper towels. Microwave, uncovered, on HIGH 4 min or until tender, rearranging slices once during cooking. Repeat with remaining eggplant.

3. Spread 50 mL (¼ cup) of the spaghetti sauce in 20 by 20 cm (8 by 8 inch) microwave-safe baking dish. Layer ½ of the eggplant, ½ of the mozzarella and ½ of the remaining spaghetti sauce in dish; repeat layers. Sprinkle with Parmesan cheese.

4. Cover with vented plastic wrap; microwave on HIGH 4 min or until hot. Rotate dish. Reduce power to 50%. Microwave, covered, 10 min or until hot and bubbling, rotating dish once during cooking. Let stand, covered, 5 min. Makes 4 servings.

■ **TIP**

If you have leftover spaghetti sauce, turn it into a quick pasta or vegetable topper. Fill a glass measure to no more than ¾ full. Cover with waxed paper or vented plastic wrap to prevent splattering. Heat on HIGH, allowing 1 minute for ½ cup, 3 minutes for 1 cup and 5 minutes for 2 cups of sauce.

Side Dishes

Vegetables in Cheese Sauce

284 mL	**can Campbell's Condensed Cheddar Cheese Soup**	**10 ounce**
75 mL	**milk**	**⅓ cup**
2 mL	**dried basil leaves, crushed**	**½ teaspoon**
1	**clove garlic, minced**	**1**
500 mL	**cauliflowerets**	**2 cups**
1	**small onion, cut into thin wedges**	**1**
375 mL	**diagonally sliced carrots**	**1½ cups**
284 g	**package frozen peas**	**10 ounce**

1. In 3 L (3 quart) microwave-safe casserole, stir soup until smooth. Stir in milk, basil and garlic.

2. Add vegetables; stir to coat well. Cover with lid; microwave on HIGH 15 min or until vegetables are tender, stirring twice during cooking. Let stand, covered, 5 min. Makes 8 servings.

VEGETABLES IN CHEESE SAUCE ▶

Cauliflower in Cheese Sauce

1	medium head cauliflower (about 1 kg [2 pounds])	1
25 mL	water	2 tablespoons
284 mL	can Campbell's Condensed Cream of Mushroom Soup	10 ounce
250 mL	grated Cheddar cheese	1 cup
125 mL	milk	½ cup
Dash	ground nutmeg	Dash
Dash	pepper	Dash
	Toasted sliced almonds for garnish (see Note below)	

1. Remove and discard outside leaves and core of cauliflower. Place whole cauliflower in 2 L (2 quart) microwave-safe casserole; add water. Cover with lid; microwave on HIGH 10 min or until tender, rotating dish once during cooking. Let stand, covered, while preparing sauce.

2. In 1.5 L (1½ quart) microwave-safe casserole, stir soup until smooth. Stir in cheese, milk, nutmeg and pepper. Cover with lid; microwave on HIGH 5 min or until hot and bubbling, stirring once during cooking.

3. Place cauliflower on platter. Spoon ½ of the sauce over cauliflower. Garnish with almonds. Serve with remaining sauce. Makes 8 servings.

NOTE: To toast almonds: In small microwave-safe bowl, combine 50 mL (¼ cup) sliced or chopped almonds and 5 mL (1 teaspoon) butter or margarine. Microwave, uncovered, on HIGH 1.5 min or until almonds begin to brown, stirring once during cooking.

Cheddar Cauliflower Casserole

284 mL	can Campbell's Condensed Cheddar Cheese Soup	10 ounce
1 L	caulifowerets	4 cups
10 mL	lemon juice	2 teaspoons
1 mL	ground nutmeg	¼ teaspoon

In 1.5 L (1½ quart) microwave-safe casserole, combine all ingredients. Cover with lid; microwave on HIGH 12 min or until cauliflower is tender, stirring once during cooking. Let stand, covered, 2 min before serving. Makes 5 servings.

Festive Cauliflower

1 L	**cauliflowerets**	**4 cups**
284 mL	**can Campbell's Condensed Cream of Celery Soup**	**10 ounce**
125 mL	**milk**	**½ cup**
125 mL	**grated Cheddar cheese**	**½ cup**
Dash	**curry powder**	**Dash**
Dash	**black pepper**	**Dash**
250 mL	**frozen peas, thawed**	**1 cup**
125 mL	**diced sweet red pepper**	**½ cup**
	Toasted sliced almonds for garnish (see Note on page 98)	

1. In 2 L (2 quart) microwave-safe casserole, place cauliflower in 1.5 cm (½ inch) salted water. Cover with lid; microwave on HIGH 10 min or until tender-crisp. Drain.

2. In medium bowl, combine soup, milk, cheese, curry powder and black pepper; stir in cauliflower. Stir in peas and red pepper. Cover; microwave on HIGH 3 min or until vegetables are tender and cheese is melted, stirring once during cooking. Top with almonds. Makes 8 servings.

Green Bean Casserole

2 (284 g)	**packages frozen cut green beans**	**2 (10 ounce)**
284 mL	**can Campbell's Condensed Cream of Mushroom Soup**	**10 ounce**
125 mL	**milk**	**½ cup**
5 mL	**soy sauce**	**1 teaspoon**
Dash	**pepper**	**Dash**
125 mL	**sliced pitted ripe olives (optional)**	**½ cup**
500 mL	**onion-ring-shaped snacks**	**2 cups**

1. Place beans in 1 L (1 quart) microwave-safe casserole. Cover with lid; microwave on HIGH 9 min or until tender, stirring twice during cooking. Drain.

2. In 1.5 L (1½ quart) microwave-safe casserole, stir soup until smooth. Stir in milk, soy sauce and pepper. Stir in beans, ½ of the olives and ½ of the onion snacks. Cover; microwave on HIGH 7 min or until hot and bubbling, stirring once during cooking. Let stand, covered, 5 min. Sprinkle with remaining olives and onion snacks. Makes 6 servings.

NOTE: You may substitute 1 L (4 cups) (about 500 g [1 pound]) fresh cut green beans and 25 mL (2 tablespoons) water for the frozen beans.

Broccoli and Celery Oriental

15 mL	**vegetable oil**	**1 tablespoon**
750 mL	**broccoli flowerets**	**3 cups**
375 mL	**thinly sliced celery**	**1½ cups**
50 mL	**sliced green onions**	**¼ cup**
25 mL	**chopped pimiento**	**2 tablespoons**
284 mL	**can Franco-American Chicken Gravy**	**10 ounce**
15 mL	**soy sauce**	**1 tablespoon**
	Cashews for garnish	

1. In 2 L (2 quart) microwave-safe casserole, combine oil, broccoli, celery and onions. Cover with lid; microwave on HIGH 4 min or until vegetables are tender-crisp, stirring once during cooking.

2. Stir in pimiento, gravy and soy sauce. Cover; microwave on HIGH 3 min or until hot and bubbling. Garnish with cashews. Makes 4 servings.

Broccoli and Cauliflower Medley

284 g	**package frozen broccoli spears**	**10 ounce**
284 g	**package frozen cauliflower**	**10 ounce**
284 mL	**can Campbell's Condensed Cream of Mushroom Soup**	**10 ounce**
75 mL	**milk**	**⅓ cup**
125 mL	**coarsely crushed onion-and-garlic flavoured croûtons**	**½ cup**

1. In 2 L (2 quart) microwave-safe casserole, combine broccoli and cauliflower. Cover with lid; microwave on HIGH 8 min or until thawed, stirring once during cooking. Drain. Cut broccoli into bite-sized pieces.

2. In small bowl, stir soup until smooth; stir in milk. Pour over vegetables. Cover; microwave on HIGH 8 min or until hot and bubbling, stirring twice during cooking. Let stand, covered, 3 min. Sprinkle with croûtons. Makes 6 servings.

BROCCOLI AND CELERY ORIENTAL ▶

Copper Pennies

1 kg	**carrots, thinly sliced**	**2 pounds**
50 mL	**water**	**¼ cup**
284 mL	**can Campbell's Condensed Tomato Soup**	**10 ounce**
125 mL	**vinegar**	**½ cup**
50 mL	**vegetable oil**	**¼ cup**
50 mL	**sugar**	**¼ cup**
5 mL	**dry mustard**	**1 teaspoon**
5 mL	**Worcestershire sauce**	**1 teaspoon**
250 mL	**thinly sliced celery**	**1 cup**
1	**medium onion, thinly sliced**	**1**

1. In 3 L (3 quart) microwave-safe casserole, combine carrots and water. Cover with lid; microwave on HIGH 10 min or until carrots are tender-crisp, stirring twice during cooking. Drain.

2. In large bowl, combine soup, vinegar, oil, sugar, mustard and Worcestershire. Stir in celery, onion and carrots. Cover; refrigerate until serving time, at least 4 h. Makes 12 servings.

Dilled Carrots and Parsnips

284 mL	**can Campbell's Condensed Cream of Celery Soup**	**10 ounce**
125 mL	**milk**	**½ cup**
1 mL	**dried dill weed, crushed**	**¼ teaspoon**
500 mL	**carrots cut into 2.5 cm (1 inch) sticks**	**2 cups**
500 mL	**parsnips cut into 2.5 cm (1 inch) sticks**	**2 cups**

1. In 3 L (3 quart) microwave-safe casserole, stir soup until smooth. Stir in milk and dill. Stir in carrots. Cover with lid; microwave on HIGH 6 min.

2. Stir in parsnips. Cover; microwave on HIGH 13 min or until vegetables are tender, stirring twice during cooking. Let stand, covered, 5 min. Makes 6 servings.

Dilled Carrots: Prepare as above, but use 1 L (4 cups) carrots and omit parsnips. Microwave a total of 19 min, stirring twice during cooking.

Citrus Squash and Carrots

284 mL	can Campbell's Condensed Chicken Broth	10 ounce
25 mL	cornstarch	2 tablespoons
15 mL	brown sugar	1 tablespoon
15 mL	frozen orange juice concentrate	1 tablespoon
Dash	ground ginger	Dash
1	large acorn squash (about 500 g [1 pound]) cooked and cut into 4 cm (1½ inch) pieces	1
4	medium carrots, cooked and diagonally sliced into 2.5 cm (1 inch) pieces	4

1. In 3 L (3 quart) microwave-safe casserole, stir together broth, cornstarch, sugar, orange juice concentrate and ginger. Microwave, uncovered, on HIGH 4 min or until mixture thickens, stirring twice during cooking.

2. Stir in squash and carrots. Cover with lid; microwave on HIGH 4 min or until vegetables are glazed, stirring once during cooking. Makes 8 servings.

Okra Creole

15 mL	vegetable oil	1 tablespoon
250 mL	sliced celery	1 cup
1	large green pepper, cut into strips	1
125 mL	chopped onion	½ cup
1	bay leaf	1
1 mL	dried thyme leaves, crushed	¼ teaspoon
Dash	cayenne pepper	Dash
284 g	package frozen sliced okra, cooked and drained	10 ounce
284 mL	can Campbell's Condensed Tomato Soup	10 ounce

1. In 2 L (2 quart) microwave-safe casserole, combine oil, celery, green pepper, onion, bay leaf, thyme and cayenne pepper. Cover with lid; microwave on HIGH 5 min or until vegetables are tender, stirring once during cooking.

2. Stir in okra and soup. Cover; microwave on HIGH 3 min or until hot and bubbling. Remove bay leaf. Makes 6 servings.

Creamy Cabbage

2 L	shredded cabbage	8 cups
284 mL	can Campbell's Condensed Cream of Celery Soup	10 ounce
75 mL	milk	⅓ cup
15 mL	vinegar	1 tablespoon
5 mL	caraway seed	1 teaspoon
50 mL	grated Parmesan cheese	¼ cup
	Green pepper rings for garnish	

1. Place cabbage in 3 L (3 quart) microwave-safe casserole. In small bowl, stir soup until smooth. Stir in milk, vinegar and caraway seed; pour over cabbage. Cover with lid; microwave on HIGH 15 min or until cabbage is tender, stirring twice during cooking.

2. Stir in Parmesan. Let stand, covered, 5 min. Garnish with green pepper rings. Makes 8 servings.

Corn Pudding

284 mL	can Campbell's Condensed Cream of Celery Soup	10 ounce
250 mL	milk	1 cup
75 mL	yellow cornmeal	⅓ cup
50 mL	butter or margarine	¼ cup
4	eggs, beaten	4
540 mL	can whole kernel corn, drained	19 ounce
125 mL	chopped sweet red pepper	½ cup
2 mL	hot pepper sauce	½ teaspoon

1. In 3 L (3 quart) microwave-safe casserole, stir soup until smooth. Stir in milk and cornmeal. Cover with lid; microwave on HIGH 6 min or until bubbling, stirring twice during cooking. Stir in butter. Let stand, covered, 5 min.

2. In medium bowl, combine eggs, corn, red pepper and hot pepper sauce. Gradually stir egg mixture into soup mixture until well blended. Cover; microwave on HIGH 6 min, stirring once during cooking. Stir again.

3. Reduce power to 50%. Cover; microwave 12 min or until knife inserted into centre comes out clean, rotating dish twice during cooking. Let stand, covered, 5 min. Makes 6 servings.

CREAMY CABBAGE ▶

Ratatouille

25 mL	olive or vegetable oil	2 tablespoons
125 mL	coarsely chopped onion	½ cup
1	medium sweet red pepper, cut into 2.5 cm (1 inch) squares	1
2	cloves garlic, minced	2
284 mL	can Campbell's Condensed Tomato Soup	10 ounce
5 mL	dried oregano leaves, crushed	1 teaspoon
1	small eggplant, peeled and cut into 2.5 cm (1 inch) cubes	1
2	medium zucchini, cut into 1 cm (¼ inch) slices	2
250 mL	sliced pitted ripe olives	1 cup

1. In 3 L (3 quart) microwave-safe casserole, combine oil, onion, pepper and garlic. Cover with lid; microwave on HIGH 4 min or until vegetables are tender, stirring once during cooking.

2. Stir in remaining ingredients. Cover; microwave on HIGH 15 min or until vegetables are tender, stirring twice during cooking. Let stand, covered, 5 min. Makes 8 servings.

Country Kitchen Ratatouille

Flavours of the Italian and French Rivieras combine in a classic dish featuring eggplant in a rich tomato sauce. Great for lunch or dinner.

50 mL	olive oil	¼ cup
1	medium onion, sliced	1
1	clove garlic, minced	1
750 mL	eggplant cubes (about 2 cm [¾ inch])	3 cups
250 mL	sweet red pepper squares (about 2.5 cm [1 inch])	1 cup
250 mL	sliced zucchini (about 1 cm [¼ inch])	1 cup
450 mL	Prego Spaghetti Sauce	1¾ cups

1. In 2 L (2 quart) microwave-safe casserole, combine oil, onion, garlic, eggplant, pepper and zucchini. Cover with lid; microwave on HIGH 10 min or until vegetables are tender, turning dish and stirring once during cooking.

2. Stir in spaghetti sauce. Cover; microwave on HIGH 3 min or until hot and bubbling, stirring once during cooking. Makes 6 servings.

Onions in Herb Sauce

6	**medium onions, peeled**	**6**
284 mL	**can Campbell's Condensed Cheddar Cheese Soup**	**10 ounce**
25 mL	**wine vinegar**	**2 tablespoons**
10 mL	**dried dill weed, crushed**	**2 teaspoons**
15 mL	**Dijon-style mustard**	**1 tablespoon**
125 mL	**sour cream**	**½ cup**

1. Cut 1.5 cm (½ inch) deep "X" in top of each onion. Place in 2 L (2 quart) microwave-safe casserole; set aside.

2. In small bowl, stir soup until smooth. Stir in vinegar, dill and mustard. Pour over onions. Cover with lid; microwave on HIGH 12 min or until onions are fork-tender, rotating dish once during cooking. Let stand, covered, 5 min.

3. Transfer onions to serving plate. Stir sour cream into sauce. Spoon some sauce over onions; pass remaining sauce. Makes 6 servings.

Zucchini Marinara

500 g	**zucchini, cut into 1 cm (¼ inch slices)**	**1 pound**
250 mL	**Prego Spaghetti Sauce**	**1 cup**
25 mL	**chopped fresh parsley**	**2 tablespoons**
5 mL	**dried basil leaves, crushed**	**1 teaspoon**
15 mL	**lemon juice**	**1 tablespoon**
50 mL	**grated Parmesan cheese**	**¼ cup**

1. In 2 L (2 quart) microwave-safe casserole, combine zucchini, spaghetti sauce, parsley, basil and lemon juice. Cover with lid; microwave on HIGH 8 min or until zucchini is nearly tender, stirring twice during cooking.

2. Stir in Parmesan. Let stand, covered, 5 min. Makes 6 servings.

■ **TIP**

If you have trouble cutting through hard vegetables such as winter squash, pierce in several places, then microwave the whole vegetable on HIGH about 1 min to soften slightly.

Fresh Vegetable Ring

This recipe demonstrates how the arrangement of food can compensate for differences in cooking time. Dense vegetables such as broccoli and cauliflower, which take longer to cook than soft vegetables, are placed around the edge of the platter where they absorb more microwave energy.

500 mL	**broccoli flowerets**	**2 cups**
500 mL	**cauliflowerets**	**2 cups**
1	**small zucchini, cut into 1 cm (¼ inch) slices**	**1**
1	**small yellow summer squash, cut into 1 cm (¼ inch) slices**	**1**
284 mL	**can Campbell's Condensed Chicken broth**	**10 ounce**
6	**fresh mushrooms, halved**	**6**
	Sweet red pepper strips for garnish	
10 mL	**cornstarch**	**2 teaspoons**
2 mL	**dried basil leaves, crushed**	**½ teaspoon**
5 mL	**white vinegar**	**1 teaspoon**

1. Arrange broccoli in circle around the rim of 30 cm (12 inch) microwave-safe platter. Arrange cauliflower next to broccoli. Arrange alternate slices of zucchini and yellow squash next to cauliflower, leaving space in center of platter. Pour 50 mL (¼ cup) of the broth over vegetables. Cover with vented plastic wrap; microwave on HIGH 5 min, rotating dish once during cooking.

2. Place mushrooms in center of platter. Garnish with red pepper strips. Cover; microwave on HIGH 2 min or until vegetables are tender-crisp. Let stand, covered, while preparing sauce.

3. In small microwave-safe bowl, stir together remaining broth and remaining ingredients until smooth. Cover with vented plastic wrap; microwave on HIGH 2 min or until mixture is bubbling, stirring twice during cooking. Spoon over vegetables. Makes 6 servings.

■ **TIP**

Don't sprinkle salt over vegetables or other foods before microwaving. The salt attracts microwave energy and can cause overcooking in spots. Instead, add salt to cooking liquid or to foods after cooking.

FRESH VEGETABLE RING ▶

Nutty Spinach Casserole

This special side dish is a good choice for a party menu, yet it's easy enough to serve on a busy week night, too.

2 (284 g)	**packages frozen chopped spinach**	**2 (10 ounce)**
284 mL	**can Campbell's Condensed Cream of Mushroom Soup**	**10 ounce**
2	**eggs**	**2**
125 mL	**grated Cheddar cheese**	**½ cup**
50 mL	**chopped green onions**	**¼ cup**
50 mL	**toasted chopped walnuts (see Note below)**	**¼ cup**
25 mL	**grated Parmesan cheese**	**2 tablespoons**

1. Place spinach in 1.5 L (1½ quart) microwave-safe casserole. Cover with lid; microwave on HIGH 8 min or until hot, stirring twice during cooking. Drain well.

2. In small bowl, stir soup until smooth. Stir soup and remaining ingredients into spinach. Microwave, uncovered, on HIGH 12 min or until set in centre, rotating dish twice during cooking. Makes 6 servings.

NOTE: To toast walnuts: In small microwave-safe bowl, combine 50 mL (¼ cup) chopped walnuts and 5 mL (1 teaspoon) butter or margarine. Microwave, uncovered, on HIGH 2 min or until walnuts begin to brown, stirring twice during cooking.

Walnut Vegetable Medley

500 g	**carrots, cut into 4 cm (1½ inch) sticks**	**1 pound**
284 mL	**can Campbell's Condensed Cream of Celery Soup**	**10 ounce**
125 mL	**milk**	**½ cup**
5 mL	**dried basil leaves, crushed**	**1 teaspoon**
750 mL	**broccoli flowerets**	**3 cups**
	Toasted chopped walnuts for garnish (see Note above)	

1. In 3 L (3 quart) microwave-safe casserole, place carrots in 1.5 cm (½ inch) of salted water. Cover with lid; microwave on HIGH 10 min or until tender-crisp, stirring once during cooking. Drain.

2. In medium bowl, combine soup, milk and basil. Pour over carrots. Stir in broccoli. Cover; microwave on HIGH 5 min or until vegetables are tender, stirring once during cooking. Let stand, covered, 5 min. Top with walnuts. Makes 8 servings.

Curried Vegetable Medley

15 mL	**vegetable oil**	**1 tablespoon**
5 mL	**curry powder**	**1 teaspoon**
1 mL	**ground cumin**	**¼ teaspoon**
500 mL	**cauliflowerets**	**2 cups**
250 mL	**green beans, cut into 2.5 cm (1 inch) pieces**	**1 cup**
250 mL	**sliced fresh mushrooms**	**1 cup**
125 mL	**diagonally sliced carrots**	**½ cup**
1	**clove garlic, minced**	**1**
375 mL	**V8 Vegetable Juice**	**1½ cups**
15 mL	**cornstarch**	**1 tablespoon**
Dash	**pepper**	**Dash**
	Toasted sliced almonds for garnish (see Note on page 98)	

1. In 3 L (3 quart) microwave-safe casserole, combine oil, curry and cumin. Microwave, uncovered, on HIGH 1 min.

2. Stir in cauliflower, green beans, mushrooms, carrots and garlic. Cover with lid; microwave on HIGH 6 min or until vegetables are tender, stirring once during cooking.

3. In small bowl, stir together juice, cornstarch and pepper. Stir into vegetable mixture. Cover; microwave on HIGH 4 min or until thickened, stirring once during cooking. Garnish with almonds. Makes 8 servings.

■ **TIP**

Do you miss the crunch of a browned topping on a casserole or vegetable dish? Add one of these just before serving to improve appearance, flavour and texture: Crushed potato or corn chips, croûtons (whole or crushed), toasted slivered almonds or chopped peanuts, crushed corn flakes or other cereal or crushed crackers (your favourite variety).

Potato and Cheese Casserole

If desired, you can leave the skins on the potatoes for a more homey casserole.

284 mL	**can Campbell's Condensed Cream of Celery Soup**	**10 ounce**
250 mL	**grated Cheddar cheese**	**1 cup**
125 mL	**milk**	**½ cup**
Dash	**pepper**	**Dash**
1	**large clove garlic, minced**	**1**
1 L	**thinly sliced potatoes**	**4 cups**
250 mL	**thinly sliced onions**	**1 cup**

1. In medium bowl, stir soup until smooth. Stir in cheese, milk, pepper and garlic.

2. In 2 L (2 quart) microwave-safe casserole, layer ½ of the potatoes, ½ of the onions and ½ of the soup mixture. Repeat layers.

3. Cover with lid; microwave on HIGH 23 min or until potatoes are tender, rotating dish 3 times during cooking. Let stand, covered, 5 min. Makes 6 servings.

Lyonnaise Potatoes

Here's a quick dish to delight those who love potatoes and gravy; the potatoes cook right in the gravy, absorbing all of its savoury goodness.

750 mL	**thinly sliced onions**	**3 cups**
1	**clove garlic, minced**	**1**
284 mL	**can Franco-American Chicken Gravy**	**10 ounce**
1 L	**thinly sliced potatoes**	**4 cups**
Dash	**pepper**	**Dash**
2 mL	**paprika**	**½ teaspoon**

1. In 30 by 20 cm (12 x 8 inch) baking dish, combine onions, garlic and gravy. Cover with vented plastic wrap; microwave on HIGH 5 min or until onions are tender, stirring once during cooking.

2. Stir in potatoes and pepper; sprinkle with paprika. Cover; microwave on HIGH 18 min or until potatoes are tender, rotating dish twice during cooking. Let stand, covered, 5 min. Makes 6 servings.

Chili Potatoes

284 mL	**can Campbell's Condensed Chunky Chili Beef Soup**	**10 ounce**
50 mL	**water**	**¼ cup**
1 mL	**ground cumin**	**¼ teaspoon**
750 mL	**thinly sliced potatoes**	**3 cups**
125 mL	**chopped onion**	**½ cup**
250 mL	**grated Cheddar cheese**	**1 cup**

1. In 2 L (2 quart) microwave-safe casserole, combine soup, water and cumin.

2. Stir in potatoes and onion. Cover with lid; microwave on HIGH 18 min or until potatoes are tender, stirring twice during cooking. Top with cheese. Let stand, covered, 5 min. Makes 6 servings.

Cheese-Stuffed Potatoes

1.5 kg	**baking potatoes (about 10 to 12)**	**3 pounds**
50 mL	**sour cream**	**¼ cup**
284 mL	**can Campbell's Condensed Cheddar Cheese Soup**	**10 ounce**
25 mL	**chopped green onion**	**2 tablespoons**
Dash	**pepper**	**Dash**
	Paprika	

1. To cook potatoes: With fork, pierce potatoes in several places. Arrange on large microwave-safe plate. Microwave, uncovered, on HIGH 17 min or until tender, rearranging potatoes twice during cooking. Let stand 5 min.

2. Cut tops off potatoes. Scoop out pulp from each, leaving thin shells.

3. In medium bowl, with electric mixer at medium speed, mash potato pulp and sour cream. Gradually add soup, onion and pepper; mash until fluffy. Spoon mixture into potato shells.

4. Arrange potatoes on large, microwave-safe plate. Sprinkle with paprika. Microwave, uncovered, on HIGH 8 min or until hot, rotating plate once during heating. Makes 10 to 12 servings.

NOTE: To prepare ahead: Prepare through step 3. Arrange potatoes on large microwave-safe plate. Cover; refrigerate. To heat: Uncover; sprinkle with paprika. Microwave on HIGH 10 min or until hot, rotating plate once during heating.

Pasta with Vegetables

5 mL	**olive or vegetable oil**	**1 teaspoon**
2	**medium zucchini, cut into 4 cm (1½ inch) sticks**	**2**
1	**sweet red pepper, cut into 1.5 cm (½ inch) squares**	**1**
125 mL	**chopped onion**	**½ cup**
2	**cloves garlic, minced**	**2**
300 mL	**Prego Spaghetti Sauce**	**1¼ cup**
125 mL	**water**	**½ cup**
50 mL	**Chablis or other dry white wine**	**¼ cup**
250 g	**thin spaghetti or other pasta, cooked and drained**	**8 ounces**
	Grated Parmesan cheese for garnish	

1. In 2 L (2 quart) microwave-safe casserole, combine oil, zucchini, pepper, onion and garlic. Cover with lid; microwave on HIGH 4 min or until vegetables are tender, stirring once during cooking.

2. Stir in spaghetti sauce, water and Chablis. Cover; microwave on HIGH 7 min or until hot and bubbling, stirring once during cooking. Let stand, covered, 5 min. Serve over hot pasta. Garnish with Parmesan cheese. Makes 8 servings.

Double Celery Stuffing

25 mL	**butter or margarine**	**2 tablespoons**
375 mL	**chopped celery**	**1½ cups**
125 mL	**chopped onion**	**½ cup**
5 mL	**rubbed sage**	**1 teaspoon**
284 mL	**can Campbell's Condensed Cream of Celery Soup**	**10 ounce**
125 mL	**grated carrot**	**½ cup**
1.25 L	**cubed day-old bread**	**5 cups**

1. In 2 L (2 quart) microwave-safe casserole, combine butter, celery, onion and sage. Cover with lid; microwave on HIGH 5 min or until vegetables are tender-crisp, stirring once during cooking.

2. Stir in soup. Stir in remaining ingredients. Microwave, uncovered, on HIGH 8 min or until hot, stirring twice during cooking. Makes 8 servings.

NOTE: To dry bread: Arrange 8 slices fresh bread in a single layer on paper towel in microwave oven. Microwave, uncovered, on HIGH 3 min, rearranging bread slices once during cooking. Let stand, uncovered, on wire rack 10 min.

Mexicali Vegetables and Pasta

Add crunch to this festive dish by sprinkling with crushed corn chips just before serving.

25 mL	**butter or margarine**	**2 tablespoons**
500 mL	**chopped zucchini**	**2 cups**
125 mL	**thinly sliced celery**	**½ cup**
50 mL	**chopped onion**	**¼ cup**
1 mL	**dried oregano leaves, crushed**	**¼ teaspoon**
284 mL	**can Campbell's Condensed Nacho Cheese Soup**	**10 ounce**
75 mL	**milk**	**⅓ cup**
500 mL	**cooked corkscrew macaroni**	**2 cups**
2	**medium tomatoes, chopped**	**2**

1. In 3 L (3 quart) microwave-safe casserole, combine butter, zucchini, celery, onion and oregano. Cover with lid; microwave on HIGH 5 min or until vegetables are tender, stirring once during cooking.

2. In small bowl, stir soup until smooth. Stir in milk. Add soup mixture and remaining ingredients to vegetables. Cover; microwave on HIGH 5 min or until hot and bubbling, stirring once during cooking. Let stand, covered, 5 min. Makes 4 servings.

Tasty Bread Stuffing

250 g	**bulk pork sausage**	**½ pound**
250 mL	**chopped onion**	**1 cup**
125 mL	**chopped celery**	**½ cup**
50 mL	**butter or margarine**	**¼ cup**
2	**large apples, cored and chopped**	**2**
125 mL	**Campbell's Condensed Chicken Broth**	**½ cup**
125 mL	**water**	**½ cup**
1 L	**package bread stuffing mix**	**4 cups**
50 mL	**chopped pecans**	**¼ cup**
50 mL	**chopped fresh parsley**	**¼ cup**

1. Crumble sausage into 3 L (3 quart) microwave-safe casserole. Stir in onion and celery. Cover with lid; microwave on HIGH 5 min or until sausage is no longer pink, stirring once during cooking to separate.

2. Stir in butter, apples, broth and water. Cover; microwave on HIGH 5 min or until apples are tender and broth is boiling, stirring once during cooking.

3. Stir in remaining ingredients. Let stand, covered, 5 min. Makes 10 servings.

Spinach and Noodles Parmesan

125 mL	**chopped onion**	**½ cup**
284 g	**package frozen chopped spinach**	**10 ounce**
284 mL	**can Campbell's Condensed Cream of Celery Soup**	**10 ounce**
125 mL	**sour cream**	**½ cup**
125 mL	**grated Parmesan cheese**	**½ cup**
Dash	**black pepper**	**Dash**
Dash	**ground nutmeg**	**Dash**
Dash	**cayenne pepper**	**Dash**
500 mL	**cooked wide egg noodles**	**2 cups**

1. Place onion in 2 L (2 quart) microwave-safe casserole. Cover with lid; microwave on HIGH 3 min or until tender, stirring once during cooking.

2. Add spinach. Cover; microwave on HIGH 5 min or until spinach is thawed; stirring twice during cooking. Stir in soup, sour cream, cheese, black pepper, nutmeg and cayenne.

3. Cover; microwave at 50% power 8 min or until hot, stirring once during cooking. Add hot noodles; toss to coat. Makes about 8 servings.

Saffron Rice

15 mL	**olive or vegetable oil**	**1 tablespoon**
2	**cloves garlic, minced**	**2**
250 mL	**regular long-grain rice, uncooked**	**1 cup**
284 mL	**can Campbell's Condensed Chicken Broth**	**10 ounce**
125 mL	**water**	**½ cup**
Dash	**saffron, crushed or turmeric**	**Dash**
125 mL	**sliced green onions**	**½ cup**
50 mL	**toasted sliced almonds (see Note on page 98)**	**¼ cup**

1. In 2 L (2 quart) microwave-safe casserole, combine oil and garlic. Cover with lid; microwave on HIGH 1 min.

2. Stir in rice, broth, water and saffron. Cover; microwave 10 min. Stir.

3. Reduce power to 50%. Cover; microwave 10 min or until rice is nearly done. Stir in remaining ingredients. Let stand, covered, 5 min or until rice is tender. Makes 5 servings.

SPINACH AND NOODLES PARMESAN ▶

Spanish Rice and Beans

284 mL	can Campbell's Chunky Chili Beef Soup	10 ounce
375 mL	V8 Vegetable Juice	1½ cups
250 mL	quick-cooking rice, uncooked	1 cup
125 mL	water	½ cup
125 mL	chopped green pepper	½ cup

In 1.5 L (1½ quart) microwave-safe casserole, combine all ingredients. Cover with lid; microwave on HIGH 10 min or until rice is done, stirring once during cooking. Let stand, covered, 5 min. Stir before serving. Makes 6 servings.

Mushroom Risotto

15 mL	butter or margarine	1 tablespoon
125 mL	finely chopped onion	½ cup
284 mL	can Campbell's Condensed Chicken Broth	10 ounce
125 mL	water	½ cup
50 mL	Chablis or other dry white wine	¼ cup
250 mL	regular long-grain rice, uncooked	1 cup
250 mL	sliced fresh mushrooms	1 cup
125 mL	grated Parmesan cheese	½ cup
	Chopped fresh parsley for garnish	

1. In 2 L (2 quart) microwave-safe casserole, combine butter and onion. Cover with lid; microwave on HIGH 3 min or until onion is tender, stirring once during cooking.

2. Stir in broth, water and Chablis. Cover; microwave on HIGH 2 min or until hot. Stir in rice. Cover; microwave on HIGH 10 min or until bubbling.

3. Stir in mushrooms. Cover; microwave at 50% power 10 min or until rice is nearly done. Stir in cheese. Let stand, covered, 5 min. Garnish with parsley. Makes 6 servings.

■ **TIP**

Each 250 g (8 ounce) package of fresh mushrooms contains enough for about 750 mL (3 cups) sliced or 625 mL (2½ cups) chopped mushrooms.

Louisiana Beans and Rice

Serve this as a side dish or in larger servings as a main dish.

15 mL	**vegetable oil**	**1 tablespoon**
250 mL	**chopped onion**	**1 cup**
1	**large green pepper, chopped**	**1**
2	**cloves garlic, minced**	**2**
2 mL	**dried thyme leaves, crushed**	**½ teaspoon**
1 mL	**dried oregano leaves, crushed**	**¼ teaspoon**
2 (455 mL)	**cans red kidney or pinto beans, drained**	**2 (16 ounce)**
284 mL	**can Campbell's Condensed Tomato Soup**	**10 ounce**
250 mL	**diced cooked ham or smoked sausage**	**1 cup**
1 mL	**cayenne pepper**	**¼ teaspoon**
	Hot cooked rice	

1. In 2 L (2 quart) microwave-safe casserole, combine oil, onion, green pepper, garlic, thyme and oregano. Cover with lid; microwave on HIGH 5 min or until vegetables are tender, stirring once during cooking.

2. Stir in beans, soup, ham and cayenne. Cover; microwave on HIGH 5 min or until hot. Stir.

3. Reduce power to 50%. Cover; microwave 15 min or until flavours are blended. Serve over rice. Makes 5 servings.

Rice Olé

284 mL	**can Campbell's Condensed Cream of Celery Soup**	**10 ounce**
250 mL	**plain yogurt**	**1 cup**
128 mL	**can chopped green chilies, drained**	**4 ounce**
50 mL	**chopped onion**	**¼ cup**
1 L	**cooked rice**	**4 cups**
375 mL	**grated Cheddar cheese**	**1½ cups**
50 mL	**grated Parmesan cheese**	**¼ cup**
	Paprika for garnish	

1. In large bowl, stir soup until smooth. Stir in yogurt, chilies and onion; stir in rice and Cheddar cheese.

2. Spread mixture evenly in 30 by 20 cm (12 by 8 inch) microwave-safe baking dish. Cover with waxed paper; microwave on HIGH 9 min or until edges are bubbling and centre is hot, rotating dish once during cooking.

3. Sprinkle with Parmesan and paprika. Microwave, uncovered, 1 min. Let stand 5 min. Makes 8 servings.

German Potato Salad

6	**medium potatoes**	**6**
6	**slices bacon, chopped**	**6**
125 mL	**chopped onion**	**½ cup**
125 mL	**sliced celery**	**½ cup**
25 mL	**all-purpose flour**	**2 tablespoons**
284 mL	**can Campbell's Condensed Chicken Broth**	**10 ounce**
50 mL	**vinegar**	**¼ cup**
25 mL	**sugar**	**2 tablespoons**
Dash	**pepper**	**Dash**
25 mL	**chopped fresh parsley**	**2 tablespoons**

1. With fork, pierce potatoes in several places; arrange in a circular pattern on microwave-safe plate. Microwave, uncovered, on HIGH 10 min or until tender, rearranging potatoes once during cooking. Let stand while preparing sauce.

2. Place bacon in 3 L (3 quart) microwave-safe casserole. Cover with paper towel; microwave on HIGH 4 min or until crisp, stirring once during cooking. Transfer to paper towels, reserving drippings in casserole.

3. Stir onion and celery into bacon drippings. Cover with lid; microwave on HIGH 3 min or until vegetables are tender-crisp, stirring once during cooking. Stir in flour until smooth. Gradually stir in broth, vinegar, sugar and pepper. Cover; microwave on HIGH 5 min or until boiling, stirring twice during cooking.

4. Meanwhile, peel potatoes if desired; cut potatoes into cubes. Stir into broth mixture; stir in bacon. Sprinkle with parsley. Serve warm. Makes 8 servings.

Souper Potato Salad

1.5 kg	**potatoes**	**3 pounds**
284 mL	**can Campbell's Condensed Cream of Celery Soup**	**10 ounce**
200 mL	**mayonnaise**	**¾ cup**
25 mL	**wine vinegar**	**2 tablespoons**
2 mL	**celery seed**	**½ teaspoon**
250 mL	**chopped celery**	**1 cup**
50 mL	**chopped green onions**	**¼ cup**
125 mL	**chopped green pepper**	**½ cup**
2	**hard-cooked eggs, chopped**	**2**

With fork, pierce potatoes in several places; arrange in a circular pattern on microwave-safe plate. Microwave, uncovered, on HIGH 17 min or until tender, rearranging potatoes once. Cool slightly. Peel if desired. Cut into cubes. In large bowl, combine soup, mayonnaise, vinegar and celery seed. Add potatoes and remaining ingredients; toss gently to coat. Cover; refrigerate until serving time, at least 4 h. Makes 8 servings.

Chicken Rice Salad with Creamy Chutney Dressing

284 mL	**can Campbell's Condensed Chicken Broth**	**10 ounce**
75 mL	**chutney**	**⅓ cup**
15 mL	**mayonnaise**	**1 tablespoon**
2 mL	**curry powder**	**½ teaspoon**
Dash	**grated lime peel**	**Dash**
1	**whole chicken breast, split, skinned and boned (about 250 g [½ pound] boneless)**	**1**
50 mL	**water**	**¼ cup**
200 mL	**regular long-grain rice, uncooked**	**¾ cup**
125 mL	**frozen peas, thawed**	**½ cup**
50 mL	**toasted chopped pecans**	**¼ cup**
	Pecan halves for garnish	

1. To prepare dressing: In small bowl, combine 50 mL (¼ cup) of the broth, chutney, mayonnaise, curry powder and lime peel. Set aside.

2. Place chicken in 3 L (3 quart) microwave-safe casserole. Cover with lid; microwave on HIGH 4 min or until chicken is fork-tender, rearranging chicken once during cooking. Remove from casserole; set aside.

3. In same casserole, combine remaining broth, water and rice. Cover; microwave on HIGH 4 min or until bubbling. Reduce power to 50%; microwave 10 min.

4. Stir in peas. Let stand, covered, 5 min or until liquid is absorbed.

5. Meanwhile, cut chicken into bite-sized pieces. Add chicken, pecans and dressing to rice mixture; toss to mix well. Cover; refrigerate until serving time, at least 4 h. Garnish with pecan halves. Makes 6 servings.

■ **TIP**

You'll notice that microwave recipes often direct you to pierce or puncture foods with a fork or skewer. Without piercing, microwaves cause steam to build up in foods. The trapped steam may cause foods to explode. Some foods that must be pierced are: Whole eggs, egg yolks, potatoes and other whole vegetables.

Oriental Black Bean and Orzo Salad

For added colour use both sweet red and yellow peppers.

284 mL	**can Campbell's Condensed Chicken Broth**	**10 ounce**
25 mL	**vegetable oil**	**2 tablespoons**
25 mL	**rice wine vinegar**	**2 tablespoons**
1 mL	**grated fresh ginger**	**¼ teaspoon**
1 mL	**hot pepper sauce**	**¼ teaspoon**
Dash	**sesame oil**	**Dash**
50 mL	**water**	**¼ cup**
200 mL	**orzo (rice-shaped pasta), uncooked**	**¾ cup**
250 mL	**canned black or kidney beans, rinsed and drained**	**1 cup**
125 mL	**sweet red or yellow pepper cut into 2.5 cm (1 inch) thin strips**	**½ cup**
50 mL	**snow peas diagonally cut in half**	**¼ cup**
25 mL	**chopped red onion**	**2 tablespoons**

1. To prepare dressing: In small bowl, combine 50 mL (¼ cup) of the broth, vegetable oil, vinegar, ginger, hot pepper sauce and sesame oil. Set aside.

2. In 3 L (3 quart) microwave-safe casserole, combine remaining broth, water and orzo. Cover with lid; microwave on HIGH 5 min or until bubbling. Stir.

3. Reduce power to 50%; microwave 10 min, stirring once during cooking. Let stand 5 min. Rinse in colander; return to casserole.

4. Stir in remaining ingredients and dressing; toss to mix well. Cover; refrigerate until serving time, at least 4 h. Makes 5 servings.

■ **TIP**

Rice and pasta need time to rehydrate during cooking. For that reason, rice and pasta take about the same amount of cooking time in the microwave oven as they do on the stove.

Pictured clockwise from top right: ISLAND BARLEY SALAD WITH SHRIMP AND SCALLOPS (see page 124), CHICKEN RICE SALAD WITH CREAMY CHUTNEY DRESSING (see page 121), ORIENTAL BLACK BEAN AND ORZO SALAD, SPICY BULGUR AND TOFU SALAD (see page 126) ▶

Island Barley Salad with Shrimp and Scallops

284 mL	**can Campbell's Condensed Chicken Broth**	**10 ounce**
15 mL	**lemon juice**	**1 tablespoon**
1	**small clove garlic, minced**	**1**
125 g	**medium shrimp, shelled and deveined**	**¼ pound**
125 g	**bay scallops**	**¼ pound**
5 mL	**Dijon-style mustard**	**1 teaspoon**
50 mL	**water**	**¼ cup**
125 mL	**pearled barley**	**½ cup**
250 mL	**thinly sliced broccoli stems**	**1 cup**
125 mL	**canned whole kernel corn, drained**	**½ cup**
50 mL	**sliced celery**	**¼ cup**
15 mL	**chopped chives**	**1 tablespoon**

1. In 3 L (3 quart) microwave-safe casserole, combine 50 mL (¼ cup) of the broth, lemon juice and garlic. Stir in shrimp and scallops.

2. Cover with lid; microwave on HIGH 3 min or until shrimp are pink and scallops are opaque. Transfer shrimp mixture to small bowl; stir in mustard. Cover; set aside.

3. In same casserole, combine remaining broth, water and barley. Cover; microwave on HIGH 5 min. Reduce power to 50%; microwave 20 min or until liquid is absorbed.

4. Add reserved shrimp mixture and remaining ingredients; toss to mix well. Cover; refrigerate until serving time, at least 4 h. Makes 5 servings.

■ **TIP**

To remove food odours from the microwave oven, place a cut lemon in a custard cup. Microwave, uncovered, on HIGH about 1 min.

Barley Salad

25 mL	butter or margarine	2 tablespoons
125 mL	barley, uncooked	½ cup
125 mL	chopped onion	½ cup
1	clove garlic, minced	1
1 mL	dried thyme leaves, crushed	¼ teaspoon
284 mL	can Campbell's Condensed Chicken Broth	10 ounce
75 mL	water	⅓ cup
1	medium zucchini, grated	1
125 mL	chopped tomato	½ cup
50 mL	chopped green onions	¼ cup
25 mL	chopped fresh parsley	2 tablespoons
15 mL	rice wine vinegar	1 tablespoon
15 mL	chopped capers	1 tablespoon
1 mL	pepper	¼ teaspoon

1. In 2 L (2 quart) microwave-safe casserole, combine butter, barley, onion, garlic and thyme. Cover with lid; microwave on HIGH 4 min or until onion is tender, stirring once during cooking.

2. Stir in broth and water. Cover; microwave on HIGH 5 min or until bubbling, stirring once during cooking. Reduce power to 50%. Microwave 25 min or until barley is tender and liquid is absorbed, stirring twice during cooking.

3. Cool slightly. Stir in remaining ingredients. Cover; refrigerate until serving time, at least 4 h. Makes about 1 L (4 cups) or 8 servings.

Chilly Corn Casserole

200 mL	V8 Vegetable Juice	¾ cup
1 L	cooked or canned whole kernel corn, drained	4 cups
250 mL	sliced carrots	1 cup
250 mL	coarsely chopped celery	1 cup
250 mL	diced green pepper	1 cup
125 mL	chopped onion	½ cup
50 mL	vinegar	¼ cup
10 mL	chili powder	2 teaspoons
10 mL	mustard seed	2 teaspoons

In 3 L (3 quart) microwave-safe casserole, combine all ingredients. Cover with lid; microwave on HIGH 7 min or until just tender, stirring once. Cover; refrigerate until serving time, at least 6 h. Makes 6 servings.

Tangy Bulgur Salad

284 mL	can Campbell's Condensed Chicken Broth	10 ounce
200 mL	bulgur wheat, uncooked	¾ cup
125 mL	chopped fresh parsley	½ cup
1	medium tomato, seeded and chopped	1
50 mL	lemon juice	¼ cup
50 mL	olive or vegetable oil	¼ cup
5 mL	dried mint leaves, crushed (optional)	1 teaspoon
1 mL	pepper	¼ teaspoon
	Lettuce leaves	
	Sliced tomatoes	
	Fresh mint leaves for garnish.	

1. In 1.5 L (1½ quart) microwave-safe casserole, combine broth and bulgur. Cover with lid; microwave on HIGH 6 min or until liquid is absorbed and bulgur is tender, stirring once during cooking.

2. Stir in parsley, chopped tomato, lemon juice, oil, dried mint and pepper. Cover; refrigerate until serving time, at least 4 h.

3. Line serving plate with lettuce and tomato slices. Spoon bulgur mixture over tomato slices. Garnish with fresh mint leaves. Makes 6 servings.

Spicy Bulgur and Tofu Salad

284 mL	can Campbell's Condensed Chicken Broth	10 ounce
50 mL	water	¼ cup
250 mL	bulgur wheat	1 cup
50 mL	lemon juice	¼ cup
50 mL	vinegar	¼ cup
50 mL	olive oil	¼ cup
250 mL	diced zucchini	1 cup
125 mL	crumbled tofu	½ cup
125 mL	sliced green onions	½ cup
125 mL	chopped fresh parsley or coriander	½ cup
5 mL	finely chopped hot pepper	1 teaspoon

1. In 3 L (3 quart) microwave-safe casserole, combine broth, water and bulgur. Cover with lid; microwave on HIGH 4 min. Reduce power to 50%; microwave 10 min or until liquid is absorbed.

2. Stir in remaining ingredients; toss to coat well. Cover; refrigerate until serving time, at least 4 h. Makes 6 servings.

TANGY BULGUR SALAD ▶

Marinated Vegetables

Here's a great way to put lots of flavour into your vegetables with very few added calories. It's great for parties too, because everything is done in advance and the vegetables marinate until you're ready to serve them.

250 mL	**carrots cut into julienne strips**	**1 cup**
250 g	**green beans, cut into 2.5 cm (1 inch) lengths**	**½ pound**
25 mL	**finely chopped onion**	**2 tablespoons**
1	**large sweet red pepper, cut into julienne strips**	**1**
1	**large zucchini, cut into julienne strips**	**1**
375 mL	**V8 Vegetable Juice**	**1½ cups**
25 mL	**vinegar**	**2 tablespoons**
15 mL	**vegetable oil**	**1 tablespoon**
5 mL	**chili powder**	**1 teaspoon**
	Salad greens	

1. In 30 by 20 cm (12 by 8 inch) microwave-safe baking dish, combine carrots, beans and onion. Cover with vented plastic wrap; microwave on HIGH 4 min or until vegetables are almost tender, stirring once during cooking.

2. Stir in pepper and zucchini. Cover; microwave on HIGH 4 min or until pepper is tender-crisp, stirring once during cooking.

3. In small bowl, combine V8 juice, vinegar, oil and chili powder; pour over warm vegetables. Cover; refrigerate until serving time, at least 4 h. Serve over salad greens. Makes 8 servings.

NOTE: Substitute one 284 g (10 ounce) package frozen cut green beans for fresh beans.

■ **TIP**

Your microwave oven makes it easy to cook faster, but how can you cool foods faster? One way is to put the warm food into a bowl, then set that into a larger bowl of ice and water. If the hot food can be stirred without changing the consistency of it (such as a soup or stew), constant stirring will help cool the food even faster. Don't stir foods that might break up and become unattractive (potato salad for example).

MARINATED VEGETABLES ▶

Sauces

Cheddar Cheese Sauce

Served over toast and sprinkled with cooked bacon, this sauce becomes a luscious, light supper or brunch entrée.

284 mL	**can Campbell's Condensed Cream of Celery Soup**	**10 ounce**
375 mL	**grated Cheddar cheese**	**1½ cups**
125 mL	**milk**	**½ cup**
2 mL	**dry mustard**	**½ teaspoon**

In 2 L (2 quart) microwave-safe casserole, stir soup until smooth. Stir in remaining ingredients. Microwave, uncovered, on HIGH 4 min or until sauce is hot and cheese is melted, stirring twice during cooking. Serve with vegetables or potatoes. Makes about 500 mL (2 cups).

Cheese Sauce Dijonnaise

284 mL	**can Campbell's Condensed Cheddar Cheese Soup**	**10 ounce**
50 mL	**milk**	**¼ cup**
15 mL	**Dijon-style mustard**	**1 tablespoon**

In 1 L (1 quart) microwave-safe casserole, combine all ingredients. Microwave, uncovered, on HIGH 2.5 min or until hot, stirring once during heating. Serve over vegetables or poached eggs. Makes 325 mL (1⅓ cups).

CHEDDAR CHEESE SAUCE▶

Creamy Hollandaise Sauce

284 mL	can Campbell's Condensed Cream of Chicken Soup	10 ounce
3	egg yolks	3
25 mL	lemon juice	2 tablespoons
Dash	dry mustard	Dash
Dash	pepper	Dash
125 mL	butter or margarine, melted	½ cup

1. In covered blender or food processor, combine soup, egg yolks, lemon juice, mustard and pepper. Blend until smooth.

2. With blender or food processor running, gradually add butter in a steady stream. Blend 3 min more or until thickened.

3. Pour sauce into 1 L (1 quart) microwave-safe casserole. Microwave, uncovered, on HIGH 2 min or until hot, stirring twice during cooking. Serve over vegetables, eggs or seafood. Makes 500 mL (2 cups).

Herb Sauce

284 mL	can Campbell's Condensed Cream of Celery or Cream of Chicken Soup	10 ounce
75 mL	milk	⅓ cup
Dash	rubbed sage	Dash
Dash	dried thyme leaves, crushed	Dash

In 1 L (1 quart) microwave-safe casserole, stir soup until smooth. Stir in remaining ingredients; mix well. Cover with lid; microwave on HIGH 4 min or until hot and bubbling, stirring once during cooking. Serve with chicken, fish or vegetables. Makes about 375 mL (1½ cups).

■ **TIP**

Glass measuring cups are perfect for microwaving sauces and other liquids. For many recipes, you can measure the liquid right into the cup, then add other ingredients and heat. Handles on the measuring cups stay cool during cooking, so they're useful for transferring foods to and from the oven.

Mushroom Mornay Sauce

284 mL	can Campbell's Condensed Cream of Mushroom Soup	10 ounce
200 mL	milk	¾ cup
1 mL	dry mustard	¼ teaspoon
1	egg	1
125 mL	grated Swiss cheese	½ cup
15 mL	grated Parmesan cheese	1 tablespoon

1. In 1 L (1 quart) microwave-safe casserole, combine soup, milk and mustard; stir until smooth. Microwave, uncovered, on HIGH 2 min or until hot.

2. In small cup, lightly beat egg. Stir some hot soup mixture into egg. Stir egg mixture back into soup.

3. Microwave, uncovered, on HIGH 2.5 min or until mixture thickens, stirring 3 times during heating. (Do not boil.) Stir in cheeses. Microwave, uncovered, 1 min more or until cheese is melted, stirring once during heating. Makes 500 mL (2 cups).

Fresh Mushroom Sauce

50 mL	butter or margarine	¼ cup
50 mL	all-purpose flour	¼ cup
284 mL	can Campbell's Condensed Chicken Broth	10 ounce
50 mL	water	¼ cup
15 mL	lemon juice	1 tablespoon
15 mL	dry vermouth	1 tablespoon
375 mL	sliced fresh mushrooms	1½ cups
25 mL	chopped fresh parsley	2 tablespoons

1. Place butter in 1 L (4 cup) glass measure. Cover with waxed paper; microwave on HIGH 40 sec or until melted.

2. Stir in flour until smooth. Stir in broth, water, lemon juice and vermouth. Microwave, uncovered, on HIGH 5 min or until bubbling, stirring once during cooking.

3. Stir in remaining ingredients. Microwave, uncovered, on HIGH 3 min or until just bubbling, stirring once during cooking. Serve with chicken or seafood. Makes about 550 mL (2¼ cups).

NOTE: For uniform pieces in record time, slice mushrooms using an egg slicer.

Madeira-Mushroom Gravy

15 mL	butter or margarine	1 tablespoon
250 mL	sliced fresh mushrooms	1 cup
15 mL	chopped green onion	1 tablespoon
284 mL	can Franco-American Beef Gravy	10 ounce
25 mL	tomato paste	2 tablespoons
15 mL	Madeira wine	1 tablespoon
Dash	dried thyme leaves, crushed	Dash

1. In 1 L (1 quart) microwave-safe casserole, combine butter, mushrooms and onion. Cover with lid; microwave on HIGH 3 min or until mushrooms are tender, stirring once during cooking.

2. Stir in remaining ingredients. Cover; microwave on HIGH 3 min or until hot and bubbling. Serve with beef or pork. Makes about 500 mL (2 cups).

Mushroom-Apricot Sauce

284 mL	can Franco-American Mushroom Gravy	10 ounce
125 mL	apricot or peach jam	½ cup
25 mL	lemon juice	2 tablespoons
5 mL	Dijon-style mustard	1 teaspoon

In 1 L (4 cup) glass measure, combine all ingredients. Microwave, uncovered, on HIGH 4 min or until jam is melted, stirring once during heating. Serve with ham or meat loaf. Makes 500 mL (2 cups).

Chili Con Queso Sauce

284 mL	can Campbell's Condensed Nacho Cheese Soup	10 ounce
125 mL	water	½ cup
15 mL	chopped fresh parsley	1 tablespoon
1 mL	ground cumin	¼ teaspoon
125 mL	chopped tomato	½ cup

In 1 L (1 quart) microwave-safe casserole, stir soup until smooth. Stir in water, parsley and cumin. Mix well. Microwave, uncovered, on HIGH 3 min or until hot and bubbling. Stir in tomato. Serve with hamburgers, potatoes or other vegetables. Makes about 500 mL (2 cups).

FROM TOP TO BOTTOM: MADEIRA-MUSHROOM GRAVY, BARBECUE SAUCE (see page 136), CHILI CON QUESO SAUCE ▶

Barbecue Sauce Dijonnaise

250 mL	**chopped onion**	**1 cup**
25 mL	**vegetable oil**	**2 tablespoons**
2	**cloves garlic, minced**	**2**
450 mL	**Prego Spaghetti Sauce**	**1¾ cups**
50 mL	**red wine vinegar**	**¼ cup**
15 mL	**Dijon-style mustard**	**1 tablespoon**

1. In 2 L (2 quart) microwave-safe casserole, combine onion, oil and garlic. Cover with lid; microwave on HIGH 4 min or until onion is tender.

2. Stir in remaining ingredients. Cover; microwave on HIGH 4 min or until sauce is hot. Use to baste spareribs, beef or chicken during broiling or barbecuing. Makes 625 mL (2½ cups).

Oriental Barbecue Sauce

284 mL	**can Campbell's Condensed Tomato Soup**	**10 ounce**
25 mL	**packed brown sugar**	**2 tablespoons**
50 mL	**cider vinegar**	**¼ cup**
25 mL	**soy sauce**	**2 tablespoons**
2	**cloves garlic, minced**	**2**
2 mL	**ground ginger**	**½ teaspoon**

In 1 L (1 quart) microwave-safe casserole, combine all ingredients. Microwave, uncovered, on HIGH 6 min or until sauce is slightly thickened, stirring once during heating. Use to baste chicken, shrimp, or vegetables during broiling or barbecuing. Serve with remaining sauce. Makes 300 mL (1¼ cups).

Barbecue Sauce

284 mL	**can Campbell's Condensed Tomato Soup**	**10 ounce**
75 mL	**apricot or peach jam**	**⅓ cup**
50 mL	**water**	**¼ cup**
25 mL	**vinegar**	**2 tablespoons**
15 mL	**Worcestershire sauce**	**1 tablespoon**
1	**clove garlic, minced**	**1**

In 1 L (1 quart) microwave-safe casserole, combine all ingredients. Cover with lid; microwave on HIGH 5 min or until hot and bubbling, stirring once during cooking. Serve with hamburgers or use to baste chicken or ribs during last 10 min of barbecuing or broiling. Makes about 375 mL (1½ cups).

BARBECUE SAUCE DIJONNAISE ▶

Stroganoff Sauce

5 mL	**butter or margarine**	**1 teaspoon**
50 mL	**chopped onion**	**¼ cup**
284 mL	**can Campbell's Condensed Cream of Mushroom Soup**	**10 ounce**
75 mL	**sour cream**	**⅓ cup**
50 mL	**milk**	**¼ cup**
1 mL	**paprika**	**¼ teaspoon**

1. In 1 L (1 quart) microwave-safe casserole, combine butter and onion. Cover with lid; microwave on HIGH 3 min or until onion is tender, stirring once during cooking.

2. Stir in soup until smooth. Stir in remaining ingredients. Cover; microwave on HIGH 3 min or until heated through, stirring once during cooking. Serve with beef, rice or vegetables. Makes 500 mL (2 cups).

Cream Cheese Sauce

125 g	**package cream cheese, cut up**	**4 ounce**
284 mL	**can Campbell's Condensed Cream of Celery Soup**	**10 ounce**
75 mL	**milk**	**⅓ cup**
50 mL	**grated Parmesan cheese**	**¼ cup**
Dash	**pepper**	**Dash**

1. Place cream cheese in 1 L (1 quart) microwave-safe casserole. Microwave, uncovered, on HIGH 30 sec or until softened.

2. Stir in soup until smooth. Stir in remaining ingredients. Cover with lid; microwave on HIGH 4 min or until hot and bubbling, stirring once during cooking. Serve with vegetables, chicken or pasta. Makes about 500 mL (2 cups).

■ **TIP**

Microwave-safe plastic spoons and whisks are especially handy for recipes that require frequent stirring. You can leave the spoon or whisk right in the container during cooking.

Sauce Amandine

5 mL	**butter or margarine**	**1 teaspoon**
50 mL	**finely chopped onion**	**¼ cup**
50 mL	**sliced almonds**	**¼ cup**
284 mL	**can Campbell's Condensed Cream of Mushroom, Cream of Celery or Cream of Chicken Soup**	**10 ounces**
75 mL	**milk**	**⅓ cup**

1. In 1 L (1 quart) microwave-safe casserole, combine butter, onion and almonds. Microwave, uncovered, on HIGH 3 min or until onion is tender and almonds are lightly browned, stirring once during cooking.

2. Stir in soup until smooth. Stir in milk. Cover with lid; microwave on HIGH 3 min or until hot and bubbling, stirring once during cooking. Serve with poultry, seafood or vegetables. Makes about 375 mL (1½ cups).

NOTE: You may substitute chopped pecans or walnuts for almonds.

Tomato Cream Sauce

5 mL	**butter or margarine**	**1 teaspoon**
50 mL	**finely chopped onion**	**¼ cup**
Dash	**dried thyme leaves, crushed**	**Dash**
284 mL	**can Campbell's Condensed Tomato Soup**	**10 ounce**
125 mL	**sour cream**	**½ cup**
25 mL	**water**	**2 tablespoons**
10 mL	**paprika**	**2 teaspoons**

1. In 1 L (1 quart) microwave-safe casserole, combine butter, onion and thyme. Cover with lid; microwave on HIGH 3 min or until onion is tender, stirring once during cooking.

2. Stir in remaining ingredients until smooth. Cover; microwave on HIGH 3 min or until hot, stirring once during cooking. Serve with hamburgers, pasta, chicken or vegetables. Makes about 500 mL (2 cups).

Curry Sauce

5 mL	butter or margarine	1 teaspoon
50 mL	chopped onion	¼ cup
5 mL	curry powder	1 teaspoon
284 mL	can Campbell's Condensed Cream of Chicken Soup	10 ounce
75 mL	water	⅓ cup

1. In 1 L (1 quart) microwave-safe casserole, combine butter, onion and curry. Cover with lid; microwave on HIGH 3 min or until onion is tender, stirring once during cooking.

2. Stir in soup until smooth. Stir in water until blended. Cover; microwave on HIGH 3 min or until hot and bubbling, stirring once during cooking. Serve with chicken or rice. Makes about 375 mL (1½ cups).

Bordelaise Sauce

25 mL	butter or margarine	2 tablespoons
15 mL	finely chopped onion	1 tablespoon
1 mL	dried tarragon leaves, crushed	¼ teaspoon
25 mL	all-purpose flour	2 tablespoons
284 mL	can Campbell's Condensed Beef Broth (Bouillon)	10 ounce
15 mL	Burgundy or other dry red wine	1 tablespoon
5 mL	finely chopped fresh parsley	1 teaspoon
5 mL	lemon juice	1 teaspoon

1. In 1 L (1 quart) microwave-safe casserole, combine butter, onion and tarragon. Cover with lid; microwave on HIGH 2 min or until onion is tender.

2. Stir in flour. Gradually stir in broth. Add remaining ingredients. Cover; microwave on HIGH 4 min or until mixture is bubbling, stirring twice during cooking. Serve with beef or liver. Makes about 375 mL (1½ cups).

Orange Grove Salad Dressing

500 mL	V8 Vegetable Juice	2 cups
25 mL	frozen orange juice concentrate	2 tablespoons
15 mL	cornstarch	1 tablespoon
1 mL	rosemary leaves, crushed	¼ teaspoon

In 1 L (4 cup) glass measure, combine all ingredients. Cover with vented plastic wrap; microwave on HIGH 6 min or until thickened, stirring occasionally. Refrigerate until serving time. Serve with salad greens. Makes 500 mL (2 cups).

Lemon Sauce

284 mL	**can Campbell's Condensed Cream of Chicken Soup**	**10 ounce**
125 mL	**water**	**½ cup**
5 mL	**grated lemon peel**	**1 teaspoon**
15 mL	**lemon juice**	**1 tablespoon**
1 mL	**dried tarragon leaves, crushed**	**¼ teaspoon**
Dash	**hot pepper sauce (optional)**	**Dash**

In 1 L (1 quart) microwave-safe casserole, stir soup until smooth. Stir in remaining ingredients; mix well. Cover with lid; microwave on HIGH 4 min or until hot and bubbling, stirring twice during cooking. Serve with fish or vegetables. Makes about 375 mL (1½ cups).

Savoury Orange Sauce

25 mL	**butter or margarine**	**2 tablespoons**
15 mL	**finely chopped onion**	**1 tablespoon**
Dash	**ground ginger**	**Dash**
284 mL	**can Campbell's Condensed Cream of Mushroom Soup**	**10 ounce**
5 mL	**grated orange peel**	**1 teaspoon**
75 mL	**orange juice**	**⅓ cup**

1. In 1 L (1 quart) microwave-safe casserole, combine butter, onion and ginger. Cover with lid; microwave on HIGH 2 min or until onion is tender.

2. Stir in soup until smooth. Stir in remaining ingredients. Cover; microwave on HIGH 4 min or until hot and bubbling, stirring once during cooking. Serve with vegetables, poultry or seafood. Makes about 375 mL (1½ cups).

■ **TIP**

Microwave oranges, lemons and limes on HIGH about 15 sec before juicing them. The juice will be released more easily.

Breads and Sweets

Carrot-Bran Muffins

200 mL	**V8 Vegetable Juice**	**¾ cup**
250 mL	**bran cereal flakes**	**1 cup**
375 mL	**finely grated carrots**	**1½ cups**
50 mL	**raisins**	**¼ cup**
1	**egg, beaten**	**1**
25 mL	**vegetable oil**	**2 tablespoons**
50 mL	**packed brown sugar**	**¼ cup**
250 mL	**all-purpose flour**	**1 cup**
5 mL	**baking powder**	**1 teaspoon**
2 mL	**baking soda**	**½ teaspoon**
2 mL	**ground cinnamon**	**½ teaspoon**
1 mL	**ground nutmeg**	**¼ teaspoon**

1. In medium bowl, combine V8 juice, cereal, carrots and raisins. Let stand 5 min. Add remaining ingredients; stir until just mixed.

2. Place 2 paper liners in each cup of microwave-safe muffin ring or 6 custard cups. Fill cups ½ full with batter. Microwave 6 at a time, uncovered, on HIGH 2.5 min or until toothpick inserted in centres comes out clean, rotating or rearranging once during cooking.

3. Repeat step 2 with remaining batter. Makes 12 muffins.

CARROT-BRAN MUFFINS ▶

Nacho Corn Bread

15 mL	yellow cornmeal	1 tablespoon
250 mL	yellow cornmeal	1 cup
250 mL	all-purpose flour	1 cup
50 mL	sugar	¼ cup
15 mL	baking powder	1 tablespoon
284 mL	can Campbell's Condensed Nacho Cheese Soup	10 ounce
1	egg, beaten	1
125 mL	milk	½ cup
15 mL	vegetable oil	1 tablespoon
125 mL	chopped onion	½ cup

1. Grease 22.5 cm (9 inch) microwave-safe ring pan. Dust with 15 mL (1 tablespoon) cornmeal.

2. In medium bowl, combine 250 mL (1 cup) cornmeal, flour, sugar and baking powder.

3. In small bowl, stir soup until smooth. Stir in remaining ingredients. Pour all at once into dry ingredients; stir just until flour is moistened (batter will be stiff).

4. Spread batter evenly in prepared pan. Microwave, uncovered, at 50% power 6 min, rotating pan once during cooking.

5. Increase power to HIGH. Microwave, uncovered, 4 min or until toothpick inserted in centre comes out clean, rotating pan once during cooking. Let stand 5 min. Invert onto serving plate. Makes 8 servings.

■ **TIP**

At 50% power, your microwave oven will cycle on and off. The length of this cycle varies from oven to oven and can be as much as 1 min in length (30 sec on and 30 sec off). When you use a reduced power level for less than 1 min, the results may be hard to predict because you may not be sure where you entered the cycle. Instead of using a low power level for such a short time, microwave the food on HIGH, checking frequently, or place a cup of water alongside the food to absorb some of the microwave energy.

Spiced Apple Bake

200 mL	**V8 Vegetable Juice**	**¾ cup**
750 mL	**chopped apples**	**3 cups**
15 mL	**sugar**	**1 tablespoon**
10 mL	**cornstarch**	**2 teaspoons**
Dash	**ground cinnamon**	**Dash**
Dash	**ground cloves**	**Dash**
125 mL	**quick-cooking oats, uncooked**	**½ cup**
25 mL	**all-purpose flour**	**2 tablespoons**
15 mL	**butter or margarine**	**1 tablespoon**
5 mL	**sugar**	**1 teaspoon**
Dash	**ground cinnamon**	**Dash**

1. In 1.5 L (1½ quart) microwave-safe casserole, combine V8 juice, apples, sugar, cornstarch, cinnamon and cloves. Cover with lid; microwave on HIGH 5 min or until apples are just tender, stirring once during cooking.

2. In small bowl, combine oats, flour, butter, sugar and cinnamon; sprinkle over apple mixture. Cover; microwave on HIGH 4 min or until hot.

3. Let stand, uncovered, 2 min. Makes 6 servings.

■ **TIP**

To soften butter or margarine for easier spreading, place 125 mL (½ cup) butter on microwave-safe plate. Microwave on HIGH 10 sec. To melt butter, place 25 mL (2 tablespoons) butter in a glass measure. Cover with waxed paper; microwave on HIGH 30 sec.

Tomato Soup Spice Cake

This version of our classic spice cake comes out even higher and lighter than the version baked in the conventional oven.

15 mL	**sugar**	**1 tablespoon**
500 g	**box spice cake mix**	**16 ounce**
284 mL	**can Campbell's Condensed Tomato Soup**	**10 ounce**
2	**eggs**	**2**
25 mL	**water**	**2 tablespoons**
250 mL	**sour cream**	**1 cup**
50 mL	**packed brown sugar**	**¼ cup**
5 mL	**vanilla extract**	**1 teaspoon**

1. Generously grease 3.5 L (14 cup) microwave-safe Bundt® pan. Sprinkle pan with sugar.

2. In large bowl, combine cake mix, soup, eggs and water. With electric mixer, beat 2 min or until well mixed, constantly scraping side of bowl.

3. Pour into prepared pan. Microwave, uncovered, at 50% power 9 min, rotating pan once during cooking.

4. Increase power to HIGH. Microwave, uncovered, 5 min or until toothpick inserted in centre comes out clean. Let stand 15 min. Invert onto serving plate. Cool completely.

5. In small bowl, combine remaining ingredients; stir until sugar is dissolved. Spoon over cooled cake. Makes 12 servings.

■ **TIP**

To make an upside-down hot fudge sundae: Place 15 to 25 mL (1 to 2 tablespoons) of fudge sauce in a microwave-safe serving dish. Microwave on HIGH 10 sec or until hot. Top with ice cream, nuts and other sundae favourites.

TOMATO SOUP SPICE CAKE ▶

Cheesecake Pie

90 mL	butter or margarine	6 tablespoons
375 mL	graham cracker crumbs	1½ cups
2 (250 g)	packages cream cheese	2 (8 ounce)
284 mL	can Campbell's Condensed Cheddar Cheese Soup	10 ounces
3	eggs	3
125 mL	sugar	½ cup
10 mL	grated lemon peel	2 teaspoons
25 mL	lemon juice	2 tablespoons
5 mL	vanilla extract	1 teaspoon
125 mL	sour cream	½ cup
	Chocolate Leaves for garnish (recipe follows)	
	Fruit for garnish	

1. To make crust: Place butter in 25 cm (10 inch) microwave-safe pie plate. Cover with waxed paper; microwave on HIGH 45 sec or until melted. Stir in crumbs; mix well. Press mixture onto bottom and sides of pie plate. Microwave, uncovered, on HIGH 1.5 min, rotating plate once during cooking. Set aside.

2. To make filling: Place cream cheese in large microwave-safe bowl. Microwave, uncovered, on HIGH 1 min or until softened. With electric mixer, beat cream cheese until smooth. Add soup, eggs, sugar, lemon peel, lemon juice and vanilla; beat until smooth. Microwave, uncovered, on HIGH 7 min or until mixture is hot and very thick, stirring often during cooking.

3. Pour filling into prepared crust. Microwave, uncovered, at 50% power 5 min or until nearly set in centre, rotating dish once during cooking. Let stand at room temperature until completely cool. Refrigerate until serving time, at least 4 h.

4. Spread sour cream evenly over cheesecake. Garnish with chocolate leaves and fruit. Makes 12 servings.

Chocolate Leaves: In small microwave-safe bowl, combine 2 squares semi-sweet chocolate and 5 mL (1 teaspoon) shortening. Microwave, uncovered, at 50% power 2.5 min or until chocolate is melted, stirring twice during heating. Brush a thin layer of melted chocolate on veined side of nontoxic leaf such as a rose leaf. Place, chocolate-side up, on cookie sheet lined with waxed paper. Refrigerate until chocolate is firm, then carefully peel leaf from chocolate.

OR, spread melted chocolate in a thin layer on waxed paper and refrigerate until firm but not hard. Use a sharp knife or cookie cutters to cut leaves or other decorative shapes.

CHEESECAKE PIE ▶

Party Snacks

Pickled Pepper Quiche

125 g	bulk pork sausage	1/4 pound
4	eggs	4
284 mL	can Campbell's Condensed Cream of Chicken Soup	10 ounce
125 mL	half-and-half or milk	1/2 cup
50 mL	chopped mild pickled pepper rings	1/4 cup
25 mL	chopped fresh parsley	2 tablespoons
1 mL	paprika	1/4 teaspoon
22.5 cm	pie crust, baked in microwave-safe pie plate	9 inch

1. Crumble sausage into 1 L (1 quart) microwave-safe casserole. Cover with paper towel; microwave on HIGH 5 min or until pork is no longer pink, stirring once during cooking to break up meat. Drain on paper towels; set aside.

2. In large bowl, beat eggs and soup until smooth. Stir in half-and-half, chopped pepper rings, parsley, paprika and sausage. Pour into pie crust.

3. Elevate if necessary (see page 7). Microwave, uncovered, at 50% power 22 min or until centre is nearly set, rotating dish 3 times during cooking. Let stand 10 min. Garnish with additional pepper rings. Makes 12 appetizer servings.

PICKLED PEPPER QUICHE ▶

Zucchini Quiche

Feature this crustless quiche as a brunch entrée with mixed fruit and muffins.

15 mL	**butter or margarine**	**1 tablespoon**
250 mL	**chopped zucchini**	**1 cup**
250 mL	**chopped fresh mushrooms**	**1 cup**
125 mL	**chopped onion**	**½ cup**
50 mL	**chopped sweet red pepper**	**¼ cup**
1	**clove garlic, minced**	**1**
1 mL	**dried basil leaves, crushed**	**¼ teaspoon**
1 mL	**dried oregano leaves, crushed**	**¼ teaspoon**
284 mL	**can Campbell's Condensed Nacho Cheese Soup**	**10 ounce**
3	**eggs, beaten**	**3**
500 mL	**grated Cheddar cheese**	**2 cups**
15 mL	**all-purpose flour**	**1 tablespoon**

1. Place butter in 25 cm (10 inch) microwave-safe pie plate. Cover with waxed paper; microwave on HIGH 20 sec or until melted. Brush butter over bottom and sides of plate; set aside.

2. In 2 L (2 quart) microwave-safe casserole, combine zucchini, mushrooms, onion, pepper, garlic, basil and oregano. Cover with lid; microwave on HIGH 4 min or until vegetables are tender, stirring once during cooking.

3. Add remaining ingredients; stir until well blended. Pour into prepared pie plate.

4. Elevate if necessary (see page 7). Microwave, uncovered, on HIGH 13 min or until centre is nearly set, rotating dish 3 times during cooking. Let stand 10 min before serving. Makes 12 appetizer or 4 main-dish servings.

Bullshot

250 mL	**V8 Vegetable Juice**	**1 cup**
125 mL	**Campbell's Condensed Beef Broth**	**½ cup**
125 mL	**water**	**½ cup**
10 mL	**lemon juice**	**2 teaspoons**
1 mL	**prepared horseradish**	**¼ teaspoon**

In 1 L (4 cup) glass measure, combine all ingredients. Cover with vented plastic wrap; microwave on HIGH 3 min or until boiling. Makes about 500 mL (2 cups) or 2 servings.

Mushroom and Leek Tart

15 mL	butter or margarine	1 tablespoon
500 mL	finely chopped leeks	2 cups
375 mL	sliced fresh mushrooms	1½ cups
284 mL	can Campbell's Condensed Cream of Celery Soup	10 ounce
4	eggs, beaten	4
250 mL	grated Swiss cheese	1 cup
125 mL	half-and-half or milk	½ cup
15 mL	all-purpose flour	1 tablespoon
Dash	ground nutmeg	Dash
Dash	cayenne pepper	Dash

1. In 2 L (2 quart) microwave-safe casserole, combine butter, leeks and mushrooms. Cover with lid; microwave on HIGH 6 min or until vegetables are tender, stirring once during cooking. Spoon off any excess liquid.

2. In medium bowl, stir soup until smooth. Stir in remaining ingredients and leek mixture until well blended. Pour into 22.5 cm (9 inch) microwave-safe pie plate.

3. Elevate if necessary (see page 7). Microwave, uncovered, at 50% power 22 min or until centre is nearly set, rotating dish 3 times during cooking. Let stand 10 min before serving. Makes 8 appetizer servings.

NOTE: Be sure to remove sand from leeks before chopping. To clean leeks, simply cut them in half lengthwise and rinse away sand with running water.

Spicy Warmer

500 mL	V8 Vegetable Juice	2 cups
5 mL	Worcestershire sauce	1 teaspoon
2 mL	prepared horseradish	½ teaspoon
1 mL	hot pepper sauce	¼ teaspoon

In 1 L (4 cup) glass measure, combine all ingredients. Cover with vented plastic wrap; microwave on HIGH 3 min or until boiling. Makes about 500 mL (2 cups) or 3 servings.

Poached Mussels in Red Sauce

1.5 kg	mussels (about 5 to 6 dozen)	3 pounds
25 mL	vegetable oil	2 tablespoons
50 mL	chopped onion	¼ cup
1	clove garlic, minced	1
450 mL	Prego Spaghetti Sauce	1¾ cups
75 mL	Chablis or other dry white wine	⅓ cup

1. Discard any mussels that do not start to close when lightly tapped. Scrub mussels under cold running water; remove and discard beards.

2. In 4 L (4 quart) microwave-safe casserole, combine oil and onion. Cover with lid; microwave on HIGH 4 min or until onion is tender, stirring once during cooking.

3. Stir in spaghetti sauce and Chablis. Cover; microwave on HIGH 3 min or until hot and bubbling.

4. Stir in cleaned mussels. Cover; microwave on HIGH 4 min or until mussels open, stirring once during cooking. Discard any unopened mussels. Serve with Italian-style bread. Makes 8 appetizer servings.

Sunny Sipper

375 mL	V8 Vegetable Juice	1½ cups
125 mL	orange juice	½ cup
15 mL	lemon or lime juice	1 tablespoon
15 mL	honey	1 tablespoon

In 1 L (4 cup) glass measure, combine all ingredients. Cover with vented plastic wrap; microwave on HIGH 3 min or until boiling. Makes about 500 mL (2 cups) or 2 servings.

■ **TIP**
On a cold winter night, warm up with hot buttered V8. Pour 200 mL (¾ cup) V8 Vegetable Juice into microwave-safe mug. Add 5 mL (1 teaspoon) butter. Microwave on HIGH 1.5 min.

POACHED MUSSELS IN RED SAUCE ▶

Hot Chili Dip

25 mL	**butter or margarine**	**2 tablespoons**
125 mL	**chopped green pepper**	**½ cup**
50 mL	**chopped onion**	**¼ cup**
10 mL	**chili powder**	**2 teaspoons**
540 mL	**can Campbell's Chunky Chili Beef Soup**	**19 ounce**
250 mL	**grated Cheddar cheese**	**1 cup**
50 mL	**sliced pitted ripe olives for garnish**	**¼ cup**
50 mL	**sliced green onions for garnish**	**¼ cup**

1. In 1.5 L (1½ quart) microwave-safe casserole, combine butter, pepper, onion and chili powder. Cover with lid; microwave on HIGH 3 min or until vegetables are tender, stirring once during cooking.

2. Stir in soup. Cover; microwave on HIGH 4 min or until hot and bubbling, stirring once during cooking.

3. Pour into microwave-safe serving dish. Sprinkle with cheese. Microwave, uncovered, on HIGH 1 min or until cheese is melted. Sprinkle with olives and green onions. Serve with tortilla chips for dipping. Makes 625 mL (2½ cups).

Hot Cheesy Mushroom Dip

If your prefer, simply serve this easy dip in an attractive 500 mL (2 cup) bowl and omit the bread. Use chips or fresh vegetables for dippers.

250 g	**package cream cheese, cut up**	**8 ounce**
284 mL	**can Campbell's Condensed Cream of Mushroom Soup**	**10 ounce**
50 mL	**finely chopped onion**	**¼ cup**
5 mL	**prepared horseradish**	**1 teaspoon**
25 cm	**round Italian-style bread**	**10 inch**

1. Place cream cheese in 1.5 L (1½ quart) microwave-safe casserole; microwave, uncovered, on HIGH 1 min or until very soft. Beat in soup until smooth.

2. Stir in onion and horseradish. Cover with lid; microwave on HIGH 4 min or until hot and bubbling, stirring once during cooking.

3. Meanwhile, slice off top of bread; hollow out centre of bread leaving a 2.5 cm (1 inch) thick shell. Cut top and centre of bread into cubes for dipping; set aside.

4. Place bread shell on microwave-safe plate; spoon hot soup mixture into shell. Microwave, uncovered, on HIGH 30 sec or until bread is just warm. Serve with bread cubes for dipping. Makes 500 mL (2 cups).

Guacamole-Chili Dip

1	**medium avocado, peeled, seeded and cut up**	**1**
15 mL	**lemon juice**	**1 tablespoon**
15 mL	**finely chopped onion**	**1 tablespoon**
1	**small clove garlic, minced**	**1**
1 mL	**salt**	**¼ teaspoon**
Dash	**hot pepper sauce**	**Dash**
250 g	**ground beef**	**½ pound**
125 mL	**chopped onion**	**½ cup**
284 mL	**can Campbell's Chunky Chili Beef Soup**	**10 ounce**
250 mL	**grated Cheddar cheese**	**1 cup**
250 mL	**chopped lettuce**	**1 cup**
1	**medium tomato, chopped**	**1**

1. To prepare guacamole: In covered blender or food processor, combine avocado, lemon juice, 15 mL (1 tablespoon) onion, garlic, salt and hot pepper sauce; blend until smooth. Cover and set aside.

2. Crumble beef into 1.5 L (1½ quart) microwave-safe casserole; add 125 mL (½ cup) onion. Cover with lid; microwave on HIGH 3 min or until meat is no longer pink, stirring once during cooking to break up meat. Spoon off fat.

3. Stir in soup until well blended. Spread on 25 cm (10 inch) microwave-safe platter. Sprinkle with cheese. Microwave, uncovered, on HIGH 2 min or until cheese is melted, rotating dish once during cooking.

4. Sprinkle lettuce and tomato over cheese; spoon guacamole in centre. Serve with tortilla chips for dipping. Makes 8 appetizer servings.

NOTE: Serve this hearty dip as a main dish. In step 3, divide the soup mixture into four 284 mL (10 ounce) microwave-safe casseroles. Sprinkle with cheese. Microwave, uncovered, on HIGH 3 min or until cheese is nearly melted. Divide remaining ingredients among dishes.

■ TIP

To make quick nachos: In 1 L (1 quart) microwave-safe casserole, stir together one 284 mL (10 ounce) can Campbell's Condensed Nacho Cheese Soup and 50 mL (¼ cup) milk. Cover with lid; microwave on HIGH 2.5 min or until hot and bubbling. Arrange 1 L (4 cups) tortilla chips on a platter. Pour hot soup mixture over chips and garnish with jalapeño peppers, chopped avocado, sliced olives and sliced green onions if desired.

Swiss Fondue

284 mL	**can Campbell's Condensed Cheddar Cheese Soup**	**10 ounce**
500 mL	**grated Swiss cheese**	**2 cups**
125 mL	**water or beer**	**½ cup**
2 mL	**prepared mustard**	**½ teaspoon**
1 mL	**Worcestershire sauce**	**¼ teaspoon**
Dash	**hot pepper sauce**	**Dash**

1. In 2 L (2 quart) microwave-safe casserole, stir soup until smooth. Stir in remaining ingredients.

2. Microwave, uncovered, on HIGH 5 min or until cheese is melted, stirring twice during cooking. Serve with bread cubes for dipping. Makes 500 mL (2 cups).

Pizza Fondue

125 mL	**finely chopped pepperoni**	**½ cup**
1	**sweet red or green pepper, chopped**	**1**
125 g	**cream cheese, cut into cubes**	**4 ounces**
75 mL	**grated Parmesan cheese**	**⅓ cup**
450 mL	**Prego Spaghetti Sauce**	**1¾ cups**

1. In 1.5 L (1½ quart) microwave-safe casserole, combine pepperoni and pepper. Cover with lid; microwave on HIGH 3 min or until pepper is tender, stirring once during cooking.

2. Add cream cheese and Parmesan; stir until smooth. Stir in spaghetti sauce. Cover; microwave on HIGH 5 min or until hot and bubbling, stirring once during cooking. Serve with bread cubes for dipping. Makes 750 mL (3 cups).

■ **TIP**

Use the microwave oven to defrost frozen bread dough quickly. Follow package directions or simply microwave at 50% or lower power, checking frequently.

Cheddar Cheese Ball

5 mL	vegetable oil	1 teaspoon
125 mL	finely chopped onion	½ cup
125 mL	finely chopped celery	½ cup
125 g	package cream cheese, cut up	4 ounce
284 mL	can Campbell's Condensed Bean with Bacon Soup	10 ounce
375 mL	grated Cheddar cheese	1½ cups
5 mL	Worcestershire sauce	1 teaspoon
	Chopped fresh parsley	

1. In 1 L (1 quart) microwave-safe casserole, combine oil, onion and celery. Cover with lid; microwave on HIGH 3 min or until vegetables are tender. Stir in cream cheese. Microwave, uncovered, on HIGH 30 sec or until cream cheese is very soft.

2. In large bowl, mash soup with fork. Add cream cheese mixture, Cheddar cheese and Worcestershire; stir until well blended. Cover; refrigerate until firm, about 3 h. Shape into ball; roll in parsley to coat. Serve with crackers. Makes about 750 mL (3 cups).

Ratatouille Appetizer Spread

50 mL	olive oil	¼ cup
1	large onion, chopped	1
2	cloves garlic, minced	2
5 mL	dried Italian seasoning, crushed	1 teaspoon
1	medium eggplant, (about 375 g [¾ pound]), cut into 1 cm (¼ inch) cubes	1
1	large sweet red pepper cut into 1 cm (¼ inch) cubes	1
1	small zucchini, cut into 1 cm (¼ inch) cubes	1
200 mL	V8 Vegetable Juice	¾ cup

1. In 2 L (2 quart) microwave-safe casserole, combine oil, onion, garlic and Italian seasoning. Cover with lid; microwave on HIGH 4 min or until onion is tender, stirring once during cooking.

2. Add eggplant, pepper and zucchini. Cover; microwave on HIGH 12 min or until tender, stirring twice during cooking.

3. Stir in V8 juice. Microwave, uncovered, on HIGH 3 min, stirring once during cooking. Serve with French bread or crackers. Makes 875 mL (3½ cups).

Just for Kids

Chili Dogs

284 mL	can Campbell's Chunky Chili Beef Soup	10 ounce
25 mL	water	2 tablespoons
25 mL	catsup	2 tablespoons
6	wieners	6
6	hot dog buns, split	6
3	slices process cheese, cut into triangles	3

1. In 1 L (1 quart) microwave-safe casserole, combine soup, water and catsup. Cover with lid; microwave on HIGH 3 min or until very hot, stirring once during cooking.

2. Arrange wieners on 25 cm (10 inch) microwave-safe plate lined with paper towels. Microwave, uncovered, on HIGH 2 min or until hot.

3. Place cooked wieners in buns. Spoon heaping 15 mL (1 tablespoon) of the soup mixture over each. Arrange cheese triangles over soup mixture.

4. Arrange rolls on same plate lined with clean paper towels. Microwave, uncovered, on HIGH 1 min or until cheese is melted. Makes 6 servings.

CHILI DOGS, ENGLISH MUFFIN PIZZAS (see page 162) ▶

English Muffin Pizzas

2	**English muffins, split and toasted**	**2**
50 mL	**Prego Spaghetti Sauce**	**¼ cup**
50 mL	**grated mozzarella cheese**	**¼ cup**
	Pepperoni or wiener slices for garnish	
	Sliced olives, green pepper or mushrooms for garnish	

1. Spread each muffin half with 15 mL (1 tablespoon) spaghetti sauce; sprinkle with 15 mL (1 tablespoon) of the cheese. Top with garnish if desired.

2. Arrange pizzas in circular pattern on microwave-safe plate lined with paper towels. Microwave, uncovered, on HIGH 1.5 min or until cheese is melted, rotating plate once during cooking. Makes 4 pizzas.

Souper Sandwiches

500 g	**ground beef**	**1 pound**
284 mL	**can Campbell's Condensed Tomato Soup**	**10 ounce**
5 mL	**dried oregano leaves, crushed**	**1 teaspoon**
4	**crusty rolls, split**	**4**
125 mL	**grated mozzarella cheese**	**½ cup**

1. Crumble beef into 1.5 L (1½ quart) microwave-safe casserole. Cover with lid; microwave on HIGH 5 min or until beef is no longer pink, stirring once during cooking to separate meat. Spoon off fat.

2. Stir in soup and oregano. Cover; microwave on HIGH 3 min or until hot and bubbling, stirring once during cooking.

3. Arrange bottom halves of 2 rolls on 25 cm (10 inch) microwave-safe plate lined with paper towels. Spread 125 mL (½ cup) of the meat mixture over each. Sprinkle each with ¼ of the cheese. Microwave, uncovered, on HIGH 1 min or until cheese is melted. Cover with top halves of rolls. Repeat with remaining ingredients. Makes 4 servings.

NOTE: You can also use this filling in taco shells or spoon it onto hamburger buns.

Macaroni and Cheese

284 mL	**can Campbell's Condensed Cheddar Cheese Soup**	**10 ounce**
200 mL	**milk**	**¾ cup**
500 mL	**grated Cheddar cheese**	**2 cups**
2 mL	**prepared mustard**	**½ teaspoon**
Dash	**pepper**	**Dash**
750 mL	**cooked elbow macaroni**	**3 cups**

1. In 2 L (2 quart) microwave-safe casserole, stir soup until smooth. Gradually stir in milk. Stir in cheese, mustard and pepper. Stir in macaroni.

2. Cover with lid; microwave on HIGH 10 min or until hot and bubbling, stirring twice during cooking. Let stand, covered, 5 min. Makes 5 servings.

Tomato Racer Soup

375 mL	**cooked wheel-shaped macaroni**	**1½ cups**
3	**slices process cheese**	**3**
284 mL	**can Campbell's Condensed Tomato Soup**	**10 ounce**
1	**soup can water**	**1**
Dash	**dried basil leaves, crushed**	**Dash**

1. Reserve six macaroni wheels for garnish.

2. With cookie cutter or sharp knife, cut car shape out of each cheese slice. Reserve remaining cheese; set aside.

3. In 2 L (2 quart) microwave-safe casserole, stir soup until smooth. Stir in water and basil. Cover with lid; microwave on HIGH 2.5 min. Stir in remaining cheese. Cover; microwave on HIGH 1 min or until cheese is melted and soup is hot and bubbling.

4. Stir in macaroni. Cover; microwave on HIGH 2 min or until hot.

5. Pour soup into 3 microwave-safe bowls. Arrange cheese car cutout and reserved macaroni wheels on top of each bowl. Arrange bowls in microwave oven. Microwave on HIGH 45 sec or until cheese is softened. Makes 3 servings.

Frozen Food Guide

FROZEN PREPARED FOODS AND YOUR MICROWAVE OVEN

With today's busy schedules, the frozen food section of the supermarket can be a meal planner's best friend. It can provide you with quick and delicious no-work lunches and dinners. And it can come to the rescue when you're too tired to cook, when unexpected company drops by, when you're not home to help and when the kids need to fix a quick meal.

Keeping a supply of your favourite frozen foods on hand is good meal management. With the variety of frozen foods available, you can have your choice for lunch or dinner. Your microwave oven makes these dishes doubly attractive, since it can heat them in a fraction of the conventional cooking time. You'll find that most frozen products made by Campbell Soup Company offer microwave and conventional heating directions.

To make cooking and eating frozen prepared foods even more of a pleasure, read through the ideas in this chapter. You'll find suggestions on quick fix-ups for solo dinners and party nibbles. These fix-ups are easy because they're based on convenience products. Half the work has been done for you.

When you need convenience, look to your microwave oven and the array of Swanson and Le Menu frozen products. For lunch, try Swanson Chicken Burgers or Macaroni and Cheese. For dinner, the choice is yours—traditional or contemporary, gourmet or low calorie. The Swanson traditional line still features Salisbury Steak and Fried Chicken and other long-time favourites. The Swanson Gourmet and Le Menu lines offer both contemporary and classic items, such as Le Menu Chicken Parmigiana and Gourmet Linguine with Shrimp, as well as lower calorie dinners. And to finish dinner on a sweet note, try a Pepperidge Farm layer cake or fruity chiffon cake.

Before you start, be sure to read the following helpful information on microwaving frozen foods from our Campbell Microwave Institute. These tips will guarantee your frozen foods emerge from the microwave oven perfectly done every time.

NOTES ON MICROWAVING FROZEN FOODS

Frozen foods are among the most helpful time-savers for busy people, but there are some special things to remember when using them in your microwave oven. Be sure to read and follow the directions on frozen food packages because microwave directions for frozen dinners vary quite a bit. Even within the same dinner, one component may be piping hot before another is even thawed. That's because freezing a food can affect how quickly and evenly it heats.

These different heating characteristics have been the subject of a great deal of research at Campbell Soup Company, research that translates into frozen dinners that microwave with better results. Extensive testing of these dinners is done in the research lab and test kitchen to develop package directions that will work in your kitchen. Package directions are based on results from 650- to 700-watt ovens.

Here are a few notes that our testers have found to be helpful in heating frozen foods:

The most important factors that affect the overall heating time are the wattage of your microwave oven and the starting temperature of the food. Heating directions are based on foods that are no colder than -18°C (0°F)—the temperature of a typical home freezer. If ice cream stays soft in your freezer, chances are your freezer may be warmer so your frozen foods will cook more quickly. On the other hand, if your deep freezer is colder than -18°C (0°F), your frozen foods may take longer to cook.

Placement of the frozen food container in the oven cavity can affect the way it cooks. Some people find that elevating the container on an inverted glass pie plate improves the evenness of heating, while other ovens heats more evenly with the container placed on the oven floor.

As a rule, cook only one frozen dinner at a time in your microwave oven. Otherwise, each dinner will interfere with the cooking of the other. Instead, heat the one that requires the longest cooking time first, then heat the second. If the first has cooled a bit, return it to the microwave oven for a minute's extra heating. However, if you are cooking two identical dinners and directions are given for cooking both at once, then you'll have good results heating them together.

When thawing frozen foods, such as ground beef or meats, use a low power setting for the best results. Higher settings may cause parts of food to begin cooking before the centre has thawed. Consult your use-and-care manual for your manufacturer's recommendations.

Dinner for One or Two

Eating alone or with a companion can be satisfying if you treat yourselves like company. Choose from any number of Swanson and Le Menu frozen dinners and entrées, then cook according to package directions. Meanwhile, set the table with linens and flowers. If you like, choose one of the following additions to make your meal extra special:

Swanson Chicken Mini Dips: These luscious, bite-sized chicken morsels can be removed from the package in portion sizes to suit one or two. Heat according to package directions, then drizzle melted apple jelly over top.

Vegetable Salad: Nothing says freshness like a crisp vegetable salad. Simply toss lettuce with your favourite dressing, or add cherry tomatoes, cucumber slices, green pepper strips or grated carrot for colour and flavour.

Tomato and Cucumber Salad: Top sliced tomato and cucumber with a favourite salad dressing or herbed vinegar.

Guacamole Salad: Mash a ripe avocado half with garlic, salt and chili powder to taste; spoon over lettuce and tomato wedges.

Creamy Cucumbers: Thinly slice cucumbers, then fold in sour cream or yogurt and fresh dill, tarragon or parsley.

Marinated Vegetables: Pour bottled vinaigrette or Italian salad dressing over leftover cooked green beans, broccoli, cauliflower, carrots or peas. Add fresh sweet red pepper strips or celery slices for extra crunch.

Ambrosia: For a salad or dessert, combine sliced orange and crushed pineapple; garnish with flaked coconut and maraschino cherries.

Warmed Grapefruit: Sprinkle cut edge of 2 grapefruit halves with brown sugar and cinnamon. Place on microwave-safe plates. Microwave, uncovered, on HIGH 3 min or until warm.

Ice Cream Sundae: Drizzle your favourite liqueur or ice cream topping over a scoop of ice cream and leave no doubt that you've had a wonderful meal.

Berries Supreme: Spoon strawberries, blueberries or raspberries into a dessert dish; top with a dollop of sour cream or yogurt and a sprinkling of brown sugar.

Microwave Desserts: For a satisfying end to your meal, prepare one of these quick-and-easy desserts for one or two servings:

Poached Pears

1	**large pear, peeled**	**1**
25 mL	**Port wine or créme de menthe**	**2 tablespoons**

Cut pear in half; scoop out core. Arrange both halves in 1 L (1 quart) microwave-safe casserole. Spoon 15 mL (1 tablespoon) wine over each half. Cover with lid; microwave on HIGH 3 min or until pear is tender. Let stand, covered, 5 min. Spoon liquid over pears before serving. Makes 2 servings.

Fruit and Pudding

Serve this creamy pudding over bananas, peaches, strawberries, blueberries or cherries.

25 mL	**sugar**	**2 tablespoons**
7 mL	**cornstarch**	**1½ teaspoons**
125 mL	**milk**	**½ cup**
1	**egg, beaten**	**1**
2 mL	**vanilla extract**	**½ teaspoon**
250 mL	**sliced fruit**	**1 cup**

1. In 500 mL (2 cup) glass measure, stir together sugar and cornstarch. Gradually stir in milk and egg. Microwave, uncovered, on HIGH 2 min or until bubbling, stirring twice during cooking. Stir in vanilla.

2. Divide fruit between 2 dessert bowls. Pour warm pudding over fruit. Makes 2 servings.

Apple Crisp for One

This quick dessert can also be made with a large peach.

15 mL	**butter or margarine**	**1 tablespoon**
25 mL	**dark brown sugar**	**2 tablespoons**
25 mL	**quick-cooking oats, uncooked**	**2 tablespoons**
15 mL	**all-purpose flour**	**1 tablespoon**
Dash	**ground cinnamon**	**Dash**
1	**medium apple, peeled, cored and sliced**	**1**
	Whipped cream or ice cream for garnish	

1. Place butter in 250 mL (1 cup) glass measure. Cover with waxed paper; microwave on HIGH 10 sec or until softened. Stir in sugar, oats, flour and cinnamon; set aside.

2. Place apple slices in small microwave-safe bowl. Sprinkle oat mixture over apple. Microwave, uncovered, on HIGH 2.5 min or until apple is tender, rotating dish once during cooking. Serve warm or chilled. Garnish with whipped cream. Makes 1 serving.

Party Presto

When unexpected guests descend on you, be prepared with a freezer full of party food. Leave the cooking to your microwave oven, and spend those precious last minutes readying your home or yourself. Below are some examples of festive morsels and serving suggestions.

Oriental Dipping Sauce

This sauce is great to use for dipping with Swanson Frozen Chicken Mini Dips, fish sticks, fried eggplant, zucchini sticks or onion rings.

250 mL	**V8 Vegetable Juice**	**¾ cup**
50 mL	**packed light brown sugar**	**¼ cup**
25 mL	**rice wine vinegar or dry sherry**	**2 tablespoons**
15 mL	**soy sauce**	**1 tablespoon**
15 mL	**cornstarch**	**1 tablespoon**
1 mL	**grated fresh ginger**	**¼ teaspoon**

In medium microwave-safe bowl, combine all ingredients. Cover with waxed paper; microwave on HIGH 3 min or hot and bubbling, stirring once during cooking. Serve warm with chicken, seafood or vegetables for dipping. Makes 250 mL (1 cup).

■ **TIP**

Kids take to microwave ovens faster than adults who have preconceived notions of cooking. Many parents prefer that their children use microwave ovens rather than conventional stoves, so that young cooks will not be exposed to hot burners and ovens. But there are a few guidelines that children should know before using the appliance.

- Don't operate the microwave oven when it's empty.
- Use oven mitts to remove food from the microwave oven and to rotate dishes—they can become hot.
- Check food before tasting—it may be hotter than it looks.
- Be extra careful when removing a cover from food that has been microwaved—steam from the food can burn you.
- If a recipe has a standing time, be patient. Standing time is important to complete the cooking.
- Clean up spills in the microwave oven and on the door seals as soon as they happen.

ORIENTAL DIPPING SAUCE▶

Sweet Relish Sauce

125 mL	**honey**	**½ cup**
50 mL	**sweet pickle relish**	**¼ cup**
50 mL	**Dijon-style mustard**	**¼ cup**
25 mL	**butter or margarine**	**2 tablespoons**
25 mL	**lemon juice**	**2 tablespoons**
10 mL	**cornstarch**	**2 teaspoons**

In 500 mL (2 cup) glass measure, combine all ingredients. Microwave, uncovered, on HIGH 3 min or until bubbling, stirring once during cooking. Serve warm with Swanson Chicken Mini Dips for dipping. Makes 250 mL (1 cup).

Sweet and Spunky Dip

250 mL	**crushed pineapple in juice, undrained**	**1 cup**
125 mL	**apricot jam**	**½ cup**
15 mL	**soy sauce**	**1 tablespoon**
1 mL	**hot pepper sauce**	**¼ teaspoon**
1 mL	**dry mustard**	**¼ teaspoon**

Place pineapple and juice in blender or food processor. Cover; blend until smooth. Pour into 500 mL (2 cup) measure. Stir in remaining ingredients. Microwave, uncovered, on HIGH 3 min or until bubbling, stirring once during cooking. Serve warm with Swanson Chicken Mini Dips for dipping. Makes 375 mL (1½ cups).

■ **TIP**

For best results in the least time, microwave frozen breaded fish or chicken until done, then crisp in the toaster oven or broiler for a few minutes. You'll save time without giving up any quality.

Index